1973

DATE DUE

AP 8 '81			
MY 18 8			
MY 29 87			
AP 1			
MR 14 92			

UNMARRIED HETEROSEXUAL COHABITATION

Carl Danziger

San Francisco, California
1978

Published by
R&E RESEARCH ASSOCIATES, INC.
4843 Mission Street
San Francisco, California 94112
Publishers
Robert D. Reed and Adam S. Eterovich

Library of Congress Card Catalog Number

78-62233

I.S.B.N.

0-88247-535-5

ACKNOWLEDGMENTS

I would like to express my appreciation to Professor David Popenoe. I would particularly like to thank him for his thought-provoking discussions and his consistent encouragement. It was in one of Professor Popenoe's courses, early in my graduate career, that the initial ideas for this study were formulated.

I am endebted to Robert Gutman, Joseph Conforti, and Ludwig Gusmar for their helpful comments and suggestions during the writing and rewriting of this project. A very special thanks is due to my friend and colleague Helene Raskin White, who was kind enough to carefully read and comment on each chapter.

I would like to express my gratitude to Mildred Romero for efforts in typing both the draft and final copies of the study. Of course my sincere thanks goes to the cohabiting couples who agreed to let me probe their existence. I would like to thank, as well, the many people who informally gave their time and ideas to help me better understand the subject under study.

Finally, a special thanks to my parents who have always wanted the best for me and kept asking when I would be finished.

TABLE OF CONTENTS

LIST OF TABLES

INTRODUCTION

In the late 60's and early 1970's, there developed a good deal of societal concern about the future of the traditional family unit. A White House Conference on Children reported that "America's families are in trouble so deep and pervasive as to threaten the future of our nation." (Time, Dec. 28, 1970:34) A number of national magazines have focused attention on the problems facing the contemporary American family. Time, for one, questioned the ability of the traditional family to meet the needs of its members. Many sociologists and clergymen have pointed to the erosion of family-centered activity as a source of weakness in the American family structure. Much of this uneasiness is due to a recognition of the critical signi- ficance of the family in society. As Dr. Paul Popenoe, founder of the American Institute of Family Relations, pointed out, "No society has ever survived after its family life deteriorated." (Time, Dec. 28, 1970:34)

Even the casual observer close to the college campus setting in the late 60's became increasingly aware of a growing phenomenon among college students. The time when everyone clustered in the lobby of the women's dorm just before curfew, spent a few moments kissing good night and then splitting up, he back to his dorm or apartment and she, along with the other girls (women), upstairs to their rooms, was no longer the only modus operandi of college student courtship. On March 15, 1968 The New York Times brought about "public disclosure" by presenting an overview of university couples cohabiting off campus. One result of the March 15 article was the famous (infamous) "LeClair Affair." A 20-year old Barnard coed, Linda LeClair, was living with 20-year old Columbia junior Peter Behr, off campus illicitly, and under false pretenses (as far as Barnard was concerned). The LeClair affair spread through the nation's newspapers and weeklies (e.g., The New York Times, April 18, 19, 20 and 21, 1968; Time, vol. 91, No. 51, April 26, 1968; The Saturday Review, May 18, 1968; Newsweek, Vol. 71, April 29, 1968). Miss LeClair was backed by Columbia and Barnard students. A special meeting to censure Miss LeClair was held. A protestant minister and a rabbi affiliated with the university backed Miss LeClair and her demand for relaxed housing regulations for undergraduates. The final result - Miss LeClair was censured. She was denied the use of the university cafeteria and snack bar. Fur- thermore, Miss LeClair's parents were informed of the situation.

The news media, in particular the popular press, made the public aware of this trend; however, these articles made little attempt to objectively analyze the living-together phenomenon. News articles and magazine stories were generally sub- jective accounts of a few couples. At the time of the initiation of the research for this study (academic year 1971-1972), however, relevant sociological treatment of the subject was scarce indeed.

Although research on this topic has now begun to answer some of the basic questions concerning cohabitation, much of what has been accomplished has suffered from a variety of obstacles. One major problem is that professional researchers in this area have not as yet developed a universally acceptable definition of cohabita- tion.

The unmarried couple has been referred to as: a consensual union, consensual cohabitation, convenience couples, unmarried college liaisons (unmalias), compan- ionate marriage, two-stage marriage, trial marriage, unmarried married, unmarried cohabitation, syndyasmos, and living together. Whether these terms are used by popular writers or scientific researchers, the terminology employed often provides an indication as to one's philosophical or moral orientation to the phenomenon. (Macklin, 1974:4)

For example, convenience couples or "living in sin" has a different connotation

1

than does unmarried heterosexual cohabitation. Furthermore, it is clear that the labeling process indicates to some extent an interpretation of the stability or the expectations for the relationship. The terms "trial marriage" or "two-stage marriage" indicate the testing out of a relationship with the goal of marriage in the future. However, the terms "consensual union" or "living together" do not necessarily imply that the relationship is a preparatory stage to marriage. Finally, labels such as unmarried marrieds or companionate marriage may imply a permanent stable alternative to marriage.*

Researchers also do not agree as to the amount of time a couple has to have lived together in order to qualify as cohabitants. Do couples have to live together for a week, a month, or three months or longer to be considered living together? The studies that have been completed are not in agreement on this variable. Furthermore, I found little agreement on how much time the couple must spend together to be considered a cohabiting couple. Though some researcher demand only that respondents "feel that they are living together," others set standards such as four nights a week or seventy-five percent of the time. When respondents are asked such questions as, "Are you now or have you ever lived with someone of the opposite sex without being married?" the length of time together, even the definition of living together is unspecified.

For the purposes of this dissertation it is necessary to provide a definition of the situation under study. I have used the term unmarried geterosexual cohabitation because it neither suggests a moral orientation nor presupposes a goal orientation to the phenomenon. Unmarried geterosexual cohabitation involves two cross-sex individuals, each of whom considers his/her primary residence to be the one in which they cohabit. Furthermore, they themselves must define their situation as a cohabiting relationship. This definition excludes brief sexual encounters such as the "one night stand" as well as going together relationships in which the couple does not cohabit.

Recently a number of research efforts have been completed and many are in progress. A cohabitation research group has been formed and continues to attempt to disseminate information to social scientists involved or interested in exploring the various aspects of heterosexual cohabitation. A number of short studies have been published or papers presented (e.g., Arafat and Yorburg, 1973; Berger, 1971; Clatworthy, 1973; Danziger and Greenwald, 1973; Garza, 1974; Hennon, 1974; Henze and Hudson, 1973; Johnson, 1973; Kalmback, 1973; Keller and Croake, 1973; Lyness, 1972; Macklin, 1972; Peterman, Ridley and Anderson, 1974; Shuttlesworth and Thorman, 1973; Torst, 1972, 1974; and Whitehurst, 1969, 1973, 1974).

---

*It is perhaps necessary to note at this point the absence of any examination of the common law marriage as part of this dissertation. It is an area I believe that can and should be compared with middle class cohabitation at some point in the future. For the moment, however, I have made the assumption that the differences between common law unions and cohabitation are quite significant. The dissimilarities between respondents in my study and those traditionally involved in common law arrangements include age, social class background, education, etc. It may be, of course, that an examination of the differences and similarities of these two social arrangements would be extremely useful, but that study must be left for a later point in time. The present research has as its purpose the development of an impirical understanding of young middle-class cohabitors.

This dissertation will present the findings of an exploratory study completed during 1971-1972 based on fifty unmarried couples living in the college community surrounding the Rutgers University campus, New Brunswick, New Jersey. The sample (see Chapter 2) was gathered by the informal friendships network (snowball) method and aimed at describing the characteristics of the cohabiting relationships, the individuals involved, their attitudes and expectations, and the reactions of others to that relationship. This research was focused directly on the cohabiting couple. Other researchers, however, have matched the cohabiting couple to going together or engaged couples in order to make comparisons (e.g., Johnson, 1968; Lyness, 1972). Finally, a number of social scientists have concentrated their efforts in surveying the student population concerning their attitudes about living together and their experiences in cohabitation. (See Chapter 1)

Although I review these studies in Chapter 1, it is clear that though helpful in answering some of the questions I had concerning cohabitation, the available literature did not supply a sufficient amount of information. The four major questions of interest were: (1)What are the sociological explanations for the growth of middle-class cohabitation? (2)Who are the cohabitors? (i.e., background characteristics, attitudes toward marriage, sexual fidelity, drugs, abortion, privacy, legal alternatives, children, etc.) (3)What is the cohabitation experience? (i.e., how do cohabitors define their relationship; what are their living arrangements, financial arrangements; level of sex role differentiation; the advantages, disadvantages, expectations for the future, etc.) (4)What are the sociological implications of cohabitation for courtship, marriage and the family?

The studies that had been completed were for the most part either subjective accounts of a few participants, or survey studies of large populations that failed to intensively examine the phenomenon of cohabitation. Though these studies supply rates of cohabitation, level of premarital sexual experience and duration of relationships, they failed to examine the structure and the interaction between the participants of a cohabiting relationship. Moreover, the majority of the available literature was primarily journalistic and was inadequate to suggest pertinent hypotheses to be tested.

In sum, the research serves the purpose of establishing an empirically based knowledge of the phenomenon of unmarried heterosexual cohabitation and provides the necessary experience that allows the development of hypotheses for further investigation. Furthermore, it was evident that the examination of actual instances of the phenomenon of interest was the most appropriate means of achieving these purposes.

CHAPTER I

REVIEW OF THE LITERATURE

Historical Introduction

In such articles as "Trial Marriage in the Andes" and "Trial Marriage Among the Peruvian Aborigines" Price (1965) and MacLean (1941) respectively report that the Peruvian Indians have been practicing a form of trial marriage for more than four centuries. In the older form these trial arrangements were prescribed by parents with the major purposes being to analyze the female's work capacity and the compatability of the couple. Price reports that the more modern arrangement allows for the rights of young people to select their own marriage partners, yet men still seek the type of girl that is hardworking and fully capable of handling the chores of both housework and field work. He reports that among those couples who enter trial arrangements eighty-three percent are finalized in marriage with an average premarital cohabitation of somewhat less than fifteen months. Furthermore, he notes that permanent separations following marriage are rare indeed, reporting that these take place in less than three percent of the cases. It is interesting to note that Price maintains that a major advantage to these relationships is that they smooth the transitionary period from adolescence to adulthood. The advantage being that the young couple can enjoy the social and sexual advantages of being an adult in that society without carrying the burden of full responsibility. (Berger, 1971)

In Malinowski's discussion of the sexual lives of the Trobriand Islanders he refers to the "bachelor house." He explains that it was the custom among courting couples that they sleep together and have exclusive sex prior to marriage. It is interesting to contrast their system to that of western culture. The premarital Trobriand couple was expected to have sexual relations but were not permitted to eat together or share any interests except sex. (Malinowski, 1929)

Stiles (1871) and contemporary writers, such as Scott (1960) and Fielding (1961), discussed "Bundling" which originated in Europe but was carried over to this country in the eighteenth century. In 1864 Webster's Dictionary defined bundling as follows: "To sleep on the same bed without undressing; applied to the custom of a man and a woman, especially lovers, thus sleeping." According to Henry Reed Stiles the custom of bundling was brought to America from the British Isles, Wales, Holland, Switzerland, Scotland, and Germany. In response to hard economic times--scarcity of housing facilities and minimal supply of firewood--in the cold season courting couples were encouraged to spend their time in the warmth of bed. It was understood that the couple was to remain fully clothed and that no sexual exchange was to occur. However, it is clear that among courting couples many did become sexually intimate and marriage was often the result of conception. (Stiles, 1871)

In Staphorst, Holland we find that the custom of "trial nights," an old Teutonic custom, is still practiced today. Isolated by their customs and attitudes the people of this town have continued the tradition of courting couples testing the compatability and fertility of the couple before marriage. During this final stage of courtship the male spends three nights a week with his girlfriend. The custom being that if she becomes pregnant a marriage must take place. If she does not, however, there can be no marriage. (Gibney, 1948)

The concept of trial marriage (note: not all unmarried heterosexual cohabitation is trial marriage) is not a new idea although differing formulations of the concept have been presented from time to time. Richard Lewinsohn in History of

4

Sexual Customs (1956) refers to a Saxon nobleman who, in the eighteenth century, recommended trial marriages arguing that marriage for life was a "betrayal of the self, an unnatural compulsion." His solution was the formation of temporary marriages, with contracts for designated limited periods of time. (Berger, 1971)

In twentieth century America the first to present his conceptual model of a trial marriage was Judge Ben B. Lindsey. Lindsey called his scheme "companionate marriage," and his ideas first appeared in _Redbook_ magazine in 1926. Companionate marriage maintained, of course, the goal of a traditional marriage following the trial stage. Although there was the chance that cohabitation would not lead to marriage, this aspect of cohabitation was not usually discussed. In spite of the fact that Lindsey was severely criticized, Bertrand Russell, then teaching at City College in New York, supported the companionate concept but felt it did not go far enough. Russell, in _Marriage and Morals_ (1929), suggested it would be particularly applicable to university students. He felt that academic work and sex were more easily combined "in a quasi-permanent relationship, than in the scramble and excitement of parties and drunken orgies." He believed it undesirable to marry without premarital sexual experience. Furthermore, he suggested that though marriage following cohabitation should be for a lifetime, he did not believe that it should exclude sexual relations with other. (Russell, 1929) His reward for these innovative suggestions was scandal and the loss of his teaching position at the university.

Some forty years after Lindsey's article appeared Margaret Mead suggested, again in an article in _Redbook_ (1966), a two-step marriage arrangement. The two steps in this scheme are differentiated by the level of commitment and responsibility. She argued that the first stage, "individual marriage," would be entered with a simple ceremony, demand limited responsibility, would not allow children and would be easily dissolved. The second step, "parental marriage," would be entered only following "individual marriage," would allow undertaking the responsibilities of parenthood, and would be expected to involve a lifetime commitment. Reaction to Mead's ideas ranged from those who condemned her tampering with traditional structure to those who complained that her new system had too much structure. In the end, she concluded, "It now seems clear to me that neither elders nor young people want to make a change to two forms of marriage. They want to reserve 'marriage' for a commitment that they feel is permanent and final, no matter how often the actual marriages may fail." (Mead, 1968)

There have been other attempts at structured alternatives to traditional marriage. Michael Scriven, a philosophy professor, proposed a three-stage plan: this scheme suggests that marriage involves three goals - sexual satisfaction, social security and sensible spawning. His solution was to create three types of marriage, and would impose legal waiting periods before the possibility of conversion from one level to the next. (Scriven, 1968) Virginia Satir made a proposal in 1967 at the American Psychological Association which suggested that marriage be made a statutory, five-year, renewable contract. This would provide a means for periodic re-evaluation of the marriage and would demand a positive decision to continue with the relationship or it would be terminated. (Satir, 1967)

Mervyn Cadwallader, in "Marriage as a Wretched Institution" (1966:174-175), suggested another variation of the renewable contract proposal:

Marriage was not designed to bear the burdens now being asked of it by the urban American middle class. It was an institution that evolved over centuries to meet some very specific needs of a nonindustrial society.... Marriage was not designed as a mechanism for providing friendship, erotic experience, romantic love, personal fulfillment, continuous lay psychotherapy, or recreation. Its purposes...have changed radically, yet we cling desperately to the outmoded structures of the past....The basic structure of western marriage is never questioned, alternatives are not proposed or discussed. Why not permit a flexible contract, for one or more years with periodic options to renew. If a couple grew disenchanted

5

with their life together, they would not have to go through the destructive agonies of divorce and carry about the stigma of marital failure like the mark of Cain on their foreheads. Instead of a declaration of war, they could simply let their contracts lapse and, while still friendly, be free to continue their romantic quest....What of the children in a society that is moving inexorably toward consecutive, plural marriages?....If the bitter and poisonous denouement of divorce could be avoided by a frank acceptance of short-term marriages, both adults and children would benefit. Any time spouses treat each other decently, generously, and respectfully, their children will benefit.

Although many legal structured conceptualizations of trial marriage have been suggested, no legal form of trial marriage yet exists. However, many have chosen to become involved in premarital heterosexual cohabitation and see no need for involvement by the state in their relationship. Today many young people have taken the concept of trial marriages and put these ideas into practice. Again I remind the reader that trial marriage represents only one of the possible motivations which results in premarital heterosexual cohabitation. In the review of the research which follows the focus is on young college populations. To date these are the only studies which are available; yet, they provide an appropriate base from which to explore the methodology and findings of my research.

Contemporary Studies*

In the following pages I will summarize the research that has been completed and offer information on cohabitation among the general student population. I will review the surverys which were designed to measure the attitudes and cohabitation experience of student populations and those studies which compare persons who have cohabited with those who have not. The earliest attempts in this area concentrated on surveying students who were easily accesible to those completing the research (e.g., Lautenschlager, 1972; Macklin, 1972; Shuttlesworth and Thorman, 1973; Arafat and Yorburg, 1973). However, the most recent research has been directed at obtaining more representative samples of the general undergraduate population (e.g., Macklin, 1974; Henze and Hudson, 1973; Peterman, Ridley and Anderson, 1974).

In the studies reviewed in this chapter the definitions employed vary. Naturally, these differences in definition make it more difficult to organize and interpret the research findings that are available. However, since we are still in the beginning stages of developing a generally accepted operational definition, I will present the definition employed in each study and attempt, where possible, to make comparisons which take these differences into account.

The Survey Research on Cohabitation

To examine the eight major survey research projects that have been completed on cohabitation, a table summarizing these studies has been prepared (see Chart I adapted from Macklin, 1974). In order to facilitate the discussion of these studies I will concentrate first on a research project completed by Peterman, Ridley and Anderson at Pennsylvania State University. I have chosen this study for a number of reasons: The first is that this data was gathered in the winter of 1972 during the

---

*This section of the study relies heavily on Dr. Eleanor D. Macklin's excellent review of the literature (1974), her study at Cornell, and the information she compiled in the first four issues of the Cohabitation Research Newsletter.

CHART 1. SUMMARY OF COHABITATION SURVEYS ON THE COLLEGE CAMPUS (adapted from Macklin, 1974)

Author	Region	Size of School % Male	Housing Policy	Time of Study	Type of Sample Sample Size Rate of Return	Definition	Rate of Cohabita.
Peterman, Ridley, Anderson	Northeast	22,000 UG 29,000 UG/G 66% male	Off-campus option 24-hr. visitation	Winter 1972	Stratified 2,500 UG 44%	"Are now or have ever lived w/someone of opposite sex"	33% 33% males 32% fmle.
Macklin	Northeast	11,500 UG 16,000 UG/G 65% male	Off-campus option 24-hr. visitation	Spring 1972	Stratified Soph/Senior 400 UG 75%	"Share bedroom and/or bed w/someone of opp. sex to whom not married for 4 or more nights/wk. for 3 or more months."	31% 20% males 40% fmles.
Cole$_1$	Midwest	2,000 UG 51% male	All but 10% on campus. 24-hr. visitation.	Spring 1973	Probability 200 UG 95%	Same as above.	17% 18% males 15% fmles.
Cole$_2$	Midwest	1,700 UG 53% male	On-campus. Non-coed dorms. No 24-hr. visitation.	Winter 1974	Probability 175 UG 97%	Same as above.	9%
Henze and Hudson	Southwest	30,000 UG/G 57% male	Majority off-campus 24-hr. visitation	Spring 1972	Random 350 UG/G 80%	Two unrelated persons of opp. sex living tog. w/o being legally marr.	29% males 18% fmles.
Lauten- schlager	West	24,000 UG/G 54% male	Majority off-campus Co-ed dorms on campus	Winter 1972	11 classes in Marriage & the Family-557 UG/G 91%	Two persons of opp. sex living tog. in a relatively perm. manner similar to marriage but w/o legal/relig. sanction.	25% 30% males 21% fmles.
Shuttles- worth & Thorman	Southwest	28,000 UG/G 60% male	Off-campus option 24-hr. visitation	1972	8 UG courses 431 UG/G 100%	Am or have been livng. w/person of opp. sex to whom not married.	36%
Arafat & Yorburg	N.E. Urban	13,000 UG 18,000 UG/G 58% male	Commuter	1971	Convenience 900 UG 85%	Living tog. relation- ship w/memb. opp. sex.	current 20% 23% males 17% fmles.

7

period of time in which my study was being completed. Secondly, the Peterman, Ridley and Anderson study is geographically closest to the area I studied; and thirdly, both my study and that at Penn State were based at the university and community of a state university. After presenting the major findings of the Penn State project, comparisons will be made with the other survey research on cohabitation.

The Penn State project on cohabitation involved a stratified sample of 2,500 students (1,250 males; 1,250 females) from a universe of 22,000 undergraduates (14,500 males; 7,500 females) at the university in the winter of 1972. The sample was drawn from the population of students at the University Park campus of the university. A stratified sample was selected in order to be able to make sex comparisons with approximately equal N's. Random samples were drawn from the student population and a brief self-administered questionnaire was mailed to each potential respondent. Peterman, et al., explain that the response rate (44 percent) may have been somewhat diminished by the fact that the questionnaires were mailed late in the term, shortly before final examination period. Questionnaires returned by married students were removed from the working sample leaving a total of 1,099 respondents (473 males - 44 percent, 626 females - 56 percent). These figures represent 38 percent of the original male and 50 percent of the original female sample.

All of us who are completing research must be particularly aware whether those who complete our questionnaires are representative of the large population. Peterman, et al., made a number of comparisons between the respondent groups and the total undergraduate population from which they were originally selected. They concluded that those who answered the questionnaire seemed to be generally representative of the campus, with the exception that on-campus students were somewhat overrepresented in the sample.

In the Heterosexual Relationship Survey at Pennsylvania State University the definition of cohabitation employed can be found in the question, "Are you now, or have you ever lived with (eating, sleeping, socializing at the same residence) someone of the opposite sex?" According to this definition a "cohabitant" is anyone who is now or who has ever experienced a cohabiting relationship. Importantly this definition may include those who have a stable weekend living together arrangement, stay together for short periods of time as well as those who may be cohabiting seven nights a week for a long period of time. It should also be apparent that the subjective interpretation of sleeping together does not clarify whether a sexual involvement is part of the relationship and therefore may include couples who are cohabiting but are not sexually intimate. As one can see in the table summarizing survey cohabitation studies, this definition is not strictly comparable with other studies of cohabitation.

In answering the basic question, "Are you now, or have you ever lived with someone of the opposite sex?" 360 of 1,099 (473 males, 626 females) respond positively. The Penn State Study indicates that almost exactly one-third of the respondents have had some type of cohabiting experience. Furthermore, the figures for males and females are very similar: 33.4 percent of the males; 32.3 percent of the females. The data also indicates that the percent of students having had or having a living together experience increases with class standing: for the females 25 percent of the freshmen, 26 percent of the sophomores, 32 percent of the juniors and 45 percent of the seniors experienced cohabitation. The proportion of male students were extremely similar: freshmen 19 percent, sophomores 25 percent, juniors 34 percent and seniors 47 percent.

In examining trends in the increase of this type of relationship the researchers asked during which college year students had their first cohabiting experience. The data indicates that present freshmen are five or six times more likely to have had cohanitation experience during their freshman year than those who were freshmen just four years ago. Peterman, et al., suggest that housing regulations have changed and that some seniors are transfer students from more restrictive settings, yet the change does seem significant.

Since the data collected in the Pennsylvania State University sample includes information on those who have cohabited for as short a time as one week and as long as "more than one year," it is necessary to examine in more detail the length of the cohabiting experience. It should be kept in mind as we compare the results of this study with others that 73 percent of the Penn State male cohabitors and 62 percent of the female cohabitors reported their longest cohabitation as three months or less. The authors also indicate that females are more likely than males to have experienced cohabitation of four months or longer at an earlier point in their college careers. Of the 158 men and 202 women who reported a living-together experience, the proportion that had lived together four months or longer increases with class standing. The data also reveals that although women are more likely to be involved in a longer living-together experience early in their college life, by the senior year males were as likely as females to have experienced a cohabitation of four months or longer. Twenth-seven percent of the freshmen and sophomore women, 39 percent of the women who were juniors and 55 percent of the senior women who cohabited had done so for at least four months. Of the males who cohabited 9 percnet of the freshmen and sophomores, 13 percent of the juniors and 50 percent of the seniors had a living-together experience of four months or longer.

Certainly there are a number of problems that become apparent when we attempt to compare the various survey studies which have been completed. I have already mentioned the problem of differing definitions of cohabitation. Other problems arise in that some researchers questioned graduate students as well as undergraduates; some asked only who is currently involved in a living-together arrangement rather than who has ever been involved in cohabitation. Samples were selected by different means and the time of the year in which the questionnaire was administered was not consistent. Furthermore, these surveys were completed in different settings involving differing housing regulations and student residence restrictions. However, taking all of these differences into consideration, comparisons can be instructive and revealing.

The study most comparable with that by Peterman, et al., at Penn State was a project directed by Macklin at Cornell in the spring of 1972. The Cornell Study on cohabitation involved a stratified sample of 400 selected cases from a universe of 11,500 undergraduates (7,500 males; 4,00 females). The sample included 100 respondents each of male sophomores, male seniors, female sophomores and female seniors. Letters were sent to these selected respondents requesting that they come in to complete a long questionnaire concerned with nonmarital heterosexual cohabitation. Approximately 4 percent of the total sample refused to participate, 8 percent could not be located, 9 percent agreed to participate but did not complete questionnaires, and another 3 percent were found to be improperly categorized by the computers. Therefore 75 percent of the original sample completed usable questionnaires. Of the 299 respondents who did fill out questionnaires, 14 were already married. Of those who were married, half indicated that they had cohabited before being married.

Macklin was careful to evaluate whether respondents did, in fact, approximate the Cornell student population. She also reported that since students were aware ahead of time of the purpose of the questionnaire and that the task took place under supervised conditions, that students were likely to be conscientious in answering the questions. Furthermore, since those who said they had been involved in a living-together arrangement had to fill out an additional 17-page questionnaire, respondents, she felt, would be unlikely to exaggerate their experience.

In the Cornell study the definition of cohabitation employed was "to have shared a bedroom and/or bed with someone of the opposite sex (to whom one was not married) for four or more nights a week for three or more consecutive months." According to this definition, obviously more restrictive than that used in the Penn State study, those who have a stable weekend relationship, stay together less than four nights a week or have not been cohabiting for less than three months are not considered to have experienced a cohabitation relationship. This definition, however,

does include cohabitation experiences in the past as well as cohabiting relationships in which the couple is not necessarily sexually intimate.

In the Cornell study the proportion of undergraduates having had or then having
a cohabitation experience was approximately one-third. The figures again indicate
that females are more likely than males to have been involved in a three-month or
longer living-together arrangement.

For the entire sample, 20 percent of the males and 40 percent of the females
indicate that they have had a living-together experience. Among the group of senior
respondents the data reveals that 54 percent of the females and 27 percent of the
males had at some point cohabited.

The Macklin study reveals further that women are more likely than men to have
had a higher level of sexual experience in all categories except the "one night
stand" type of relationship. For example, women were more likely to have had experienced intercourse in the last month (59 percent and 43 percent, respectively).
The Cornell study suggests that if we are interested in the nonconformist group, our
attention should be turned to a decreasing minority group on the college campus, the
virgin college women now in their senior year.

Cole (1973) replicated the Cornell study using a probability sample of 200
undergraduates at a small liberal arts university in the midwest (2,000 students, 51
percent male) in the spring of 1973. In this setting housing restructions required
that almost all students (90 percent) live in dorms or at fraternity houses on
campus; however, students did have 24-hour visitation rights. In this study Cole
reports that of the 95 percent who returned questionnaires, using the definition employed at Cornell, 18 percent of the men and 15 percent of the women had been or were
involved in a cohabitation situation.

In a second institution, this one somewhat smaller (1,700 students, 53 percent
male), also a liberal arts college in the same geographic area, Cole found a somewhat different proportion of students experiencing cohabitation. This study completed
in the winter of 1974 found that only 9 percent of the sample had been or were then
experiencing a living-together arrangement. Cole points out an important factor is
that at this institution all students are required to live on campus in single-sex
dormitories and that only one senior dorm allows 24-hour visitation. He reports that
visitors of the opposite sex in all other dormitories are restricted to three hours
in the afternoon. Interestingly the same level of nonvirginity (about 60 percent)
was found at both institutions.

At Arizona State University (30,000 students, 57 percent male) Lura Henze and
John Hudson (1974) examined the incidence of cohabitation among a random sample of
graduate and undergraduate students. The data were gathered during the academic year
1971-72 through the use of structured interviews. The definition of cohabitation employed was "two unrelated persons of the opposite sex living together without being
legally married." Therefore, no time restriction is placed on the relationships and
respondents make a subjective determination as to whether or not they are "living
together." A random sample was selected from the student directory and 291 interviews
(174 males, 117 females) were completed. Twenty percent of the selected sample were
not interviewed. Henze and Hudson report that some had dropped out of school, some
could not be located and others refused to participate.

The researchers report that 29 percent of the males and 18 percent of the females
indicated cohabitation experience. A couple of points to be kept in mind for comparison to other studies are that this study involves graduate and undergraduate
(median age 23 - males, 21 - females) and that the majority of the student body does
ot live on campus.

Another study completed during the winter of 1972 was a survey of graduate and
undergraduate students at California State University at Northridge (24,000 students,
54 percent male). The housing situation at Northridge demands that the vast majority
of students live off campus; furthermore, the two dormitories available are both
coed. Lautenschlager (1972) drew her sample from graduate and undergraduate students

enrolled in marriage and the family courses.

Ninety-three percent (519) of the 557 students returned usable questionnaires. The definition of cohabitation, different from any of the other studies, was "two persons of the opposite sex living together in a relatively permanent manner similar in many respects to marriage but without legal or religious sanction." Lautenschlager found that 25 percent of the students surveyed had been or were then involved in a "consensual union." Males (30 percent) were more likely than females (21 percent) to have responded affirmatively to having experienced cohabitation. Her data indicates that of the entire sample approximately 10 percent (10 percent of the males, 9 percent of the females) were currently involved in a living-together situation.

At the University of Texas at Austin (28,000 students, 60 percent men) Shuttlesworth and Thorman (1973) surveyed both graduates and undergraduates. Whereas Lautenschlager sampled only students enrolled in marriage and family courses, the study at the University of Texas was comprised of students who were in undergraduate courses in government, English, history, journalism, and business on the day the survey was completed. University of Texas allows all students the privilege of living off campus, allows 24-hour visitation and has some coed dorms. The definition of cohabitation in this study was "living with a person of the opposite sex to whom you are not married." Again, this definition allows for a wide range of subjective interpretations. However, the researchers report that of the 431 students who completed questionnaires, 155 or 36 percent answered that they were now or had been involved in a living-together arrangement.

Finally, at City College of the City University of New York, where there are 18,000 students including 13,000 undergraduates (58 percent male), Arafat and Yorburg (1973) conducted a study on living together in 1971. City College is an urban commuter school with a large minority population. Student aides were asked to distribute the questionnaire to as wide a range of students as possible. A total of 900 questionnaires were distributed. Approximately 85 percent (762) were returned and the authors satisfied themselves that these students were generally representative of the total student population. The definition employed was somewhat vague, "living-together relationship with a member of the opposite sex" with no length of time specified. Their data reveals that approximately one-fifth of these students were currently engaged in a living-together relationship. Males were slightly more likely than females to indicate cohabitation experience (males 23 percent, females 17 percent).

A review of the table summarizing survey data on unmarried cohabitation reveals a number of interesting findings. These eight studies encompassing various geographic areas and a wide range of educational settings, from small liberal arts college to large urban university, reveal that premarital heterosexual cohabitation is not a phenomenon that is limited to one geographic area (although the rates of cohabitation are lowest in the Midwest), or one type of educational setting. Though definitions employed are not strictly comparable, it appears that on every campus there are a large number of students who have experienced cohabitation and that the level of experience increased with class standing. In these studies the percentage of students involved in a living-together situation ranged from a low of 9 percent at a small midwestern liberal arts school with conservative housing restrictions, to a high of 40 percent for females at a large university in the northeast with liberal residence regulations.

In all but the Cornell study males were somewhat more likely than females to have cohabitation experience; however, the data also suggest that where we confine our definition of cohabitation to those living together three months or longer, an equalization of the proportion of males and females cohabiting is apparent. It is worthwhile to examine the Cornell study somewhat more intensively as a kind of deviant case analysis. Here we find more females than males involved in (longer than three months) cohabitation.

11

One might suggest that the reason for the higher proportion of female cohabitants can be explained by the fact that males outnumber females on the campus by nearly two to one. However, Penn State, with a similar male/female ratio and similar residential restrictions using a more liberal definition of cohabitation, shows a lower rate of female cohabitation. Therefore, we must look elsewhere for the causal factors producing higher rates of cohabitation among Cornell women. Macklin indicates in her study that the female respondents in the sample (and generally at Cornell) are likely to come from large cities or suburbs of large cities rather than rural areas or small towns. They are very likely to have come families in which both parents have had a college education and often post-graduate education. Finally, a high proportion of her female respondents (37 percent) are from Jewish homes. These factors, Macklin suggests, are likely to combine to produce the less traditional woman. Furthermore, the atmosphere at Cornell may also play a role in that it was one of the first institutions to introduce a Women's Studies Program and to encourage a breakdown of social restirctions on women generally.

Another aspect of the level of cohabitation that becomes apparent from these studies is that housing policies and regulations on the college campus play a determining role in the availability of petential heterosexual partners. On those campuses where 24-hour visitation is permitted, obviously the potential for these visits to develop into a living-together arrangement is far greater than when students live in single-sex dorms with curfews and nightly checks.

Though these studies hardly cover the entire range of college settings, it is clear to college administrators and researchers that premarital heterosexual cohabitation is becoming a common phenomenon within that milieu. There is, however, very little information on the level of cohabitation outside the college community. The figures from the Census Bureau indicate that more people are "living together" now than ever before, or at least more are willing to admit it. In the 1970 census, 143,000 unmarried persons reported they were living with a partner of the opposite sex, while in 1960 only 17,000 indicated a cohabiting living arrangement. (Satire, 1973) It would appear that noncollege youth, older retired couples and divorced middle-aged couples are also among the ranks of the cohabitors.

Comparisons Between Cohabiting
And Noncohabiting Students
Another major aspect of cohabitation which has been the focus of research in the field is the comparison of cohabiting students with noncohabiting students. Many of those who completed surveys of living-together arrangements included a number of variables on which to examine the differences between those who do and those who do not cohabit. These variables include a number of factors related to: university status (grade point average, type of residence, class standing, field of study); family background (mother: education, occupation; father: education, occupation; family income, type of discipline, church preference); community background (hometown size, location); interpersonal relationships and experience (personal adjustment, virginity, friends); and attitudes concerning cohabitation, marriage, drugs, and heterosexual relationships.

In the Penn State study Peterman, et al.,(1974:349-350), found that grade point average was not a factor by which one could differentiate between students who did or did not cohabit: they did, however, find a relationship between field of study and tendency to cohabit.

Male cohabitors are less likely to be enrolled in physical science; female cohabitors are more likely to be in the social/behavioral science or fine/performing arts, and less likely to be in education.

The variable that showed the strongest correlation with likelihood of cohabitation was type of residence. For both males and females, they suggest, "the likelihood of cohabitation is greatly increased if the student lives off campus." (Of course, students may be moving off campus in order to cohabit rather than moving off campus

12

and then becoming involved in a cohabitation relationship.) A female dorm resident, according to the Penn State study, as about a 25 percent probability of being a cohabitor; however, the off-campus resident has better than 50 percent chance of having had cohabiting experience. The research at Penn also tested the relationship between means of financial support and likelihood of cohabiting experience, but apparently there was no significant correlation between these variables for either males or females.

In their assessment of the relationship between cohabitation experience and family and community background, the data revealed no difference between the cohabiting and noncohabiting groups on the following variables: educational level attained by parents, occupational status of parents, or lize of students' hometown. Family income was somewhat related to tendency to cohabit for males. In the Penn State study male students whose family income was less than $4,000 represents only 2 percent of the noncohabitors but 7 percent of the cohabiting males; whereas those from upper-middle income ($14,000 to $19,000) families represent 23 percent of the noncohabitors but only 18 percent of the cohabiting male students. Among the males, religious backgrounds did not differentiate the two groups; but for females this study revealed a "disproportionately high number of Catholic women reporting cohabiting experience and a disproportionately low number of Protestant women having cohabited." (Peterman, et al., 1974:350) Protestant females accounted for 47 percent of the noncohabitors but only 32 percent of those with cohabitation experience, while the Catholic females represented 43 percent of the cohabitors but only 34 percent of the noncohabiting female students.

Peterman, et al., asked respondents questions concerning their friendship patterns, level of satisfaction in their most significant heterosexual relationship, and to evualuate their level of personal adjustment. The data reveals that cohabitors report a somewhat higher level of personal adjustment and higher evaluations of the quality (closeness, openness, need satisfaction, sexual attractiveness, sexual satisfaction) of their most significant heterosexual relationship. (The researchers developed a five point scale on each of the above items.) However, differences between the noncohabiting and cohabiting groups were not significant in terms of numbers of close friends and acquaintances they reported.

The Penn State research also looked into the future and asked all respondents what type of living arrangements they would prefer following graduation from college. The choices offered included: "(a) marriage; (b) living with someone of the opposite sex but not married; (c) group marriage or communal arrangement; (d) live with someone of the same sex; (e) live alone; (f) shifting pattern perhaps involving several of the above." Respondents were asked to rank their choices 1 through 6. Analysis of this data reveals that marriage was the most popular choice for all groups except cohabiting males; and although cohabiting males were most likely to choose cohabitation as their first choice, marriage was their second most likely choice among the alternatives offered. This situation was just the reverse for female cohabitors who, on the average, were slightly more likely to choose marriage over cohabitation as "best" living arrangement following the cap and gown ceremony. The comparisons between the cohabiting and noncohabiting groups reveal the "cohabitors had a lower preference for marriage, a higher prererence for cohabitation, a higher preference for communal arrangements, a lower preference for solitary living, and a higher preference for a shifting pattern." (Peterman, et al., 1974:351) The data also reveals that male cohabitors are the least likely to seek any change in their living arrangements and female noncohabitors are the most likely to desire marriage. Finally, it is interesting to note that all groups gave lowest preference to the group marriage or communal arrangement choice.

The Cornell study (Macklin, 1974:16-20) also attempted to examine factors which might differentiate between cohabiting and noncohabiting students. Macklin found, as did Peterman, et al., a correlation between field of study and tendency to cohabit. Those students involved in the Human Ecology and Arts and Sciences programs were most likely to have cohabitation experience (approximately 40 percent) while Engineering students were least likely to have cohabited (5 percent). Among senior respondents the differences become even more striking: in the Arts and Sciences program where approximately equal numbers of males and females are enrolled, almost 60 percent of both males and females had experienced cohabitation. However, among the male senior Engineering students (females represent approximately 5 percent of all Engineering students), not even one student indicated that he had cohabited. In the Human Ecology school where females represent 80 percent of the enrolled students, approximately 45 percent of the seniors had had living-together experience. This data suggests that male/female ratio in the courses one takes may be strongly correlated with tendency to cohabit. The causal factor could be differential opportunity as well as differences in personalities attracted to the various academic programs.

Macklin and her assistants included questions in the area of family background concerning religion at birth, present religious preference, family stability, perceived success of parents' marriage, and parents' income and education level. The Cornell data reveals that present religious preference can be significantly related, for the sample, to likelihood of cohabitation experience. The group indicating no present religious preference was most likely (44 percent) to have cohabited. The data also indicated a relationship between those who indicated a religious preference and tendency to cohabit. Ten percent of the Protestants, 12 percent of the Catholics, and 36 percent of the Jewish students revealed that they had been or were now involved in a living-together relationship.

Although present religious preference was found to be correlated with cohabitation, other family background variables did not reveal significant differences between cohabitors and noncohabitors. Neither family breakup nor perceived success of parents' marriage was related to tendency to cohabit. Parents' educational levels and income levels also were not factors that showed any significant correlation to cohabitation experience.

The Cornell questionnaire included items which attempted to examine the attitudes on sexual behavior, perception of friends behavior, and actual sexual conduct and related these variables to likelihood of cohabitation experience. The data sutgests that cohabitants and noncohabitants have differential association groups and are likely to have friends whose attitude and behavior is similar to their own. Those who cohabited were more likely to report their friends having had intercourse or cohabiting experience than those who had not cohabited. Eighty percent of the cohabitants, but only 47 percent of the noncohabitants, reported that most or all of their friends had sexual intercourse; and 25 percent of the cohabitants, but only 4 percent of the noncohabitants, indicated that most or all of their friends had cohabited. Cohabitants and noncohabitants also tended to perceive their own norms as reflective of campus standards. Cohabitors predicted less virginity and greater cohabitation on the campus than did the noncohabitors. They were more liberal in their attitudes toward premarital sex than the noncohabitors and had significantly more actual experience. Whereas 100 percent of the cohabitors were nonvirgins, 32 percent of the noncohabitors had never experienced sexual intercourse. It is, of course, difficult to evaluate the causal factors in this area. Did attitudes change during cohabitation or were these attitudes present prior to the opportunity and experience of cohabitation.

As in the Penn State study, the questionnaire included items on scholastic standing and on subjective evaluations of personal adjustment. In this project, as in the Penn State study, grade point average showed no correlation with tendency to cohabit. The data also reflects agreement with the Penn State findings on level of personal adjustment and higher ratings of heterosexual relationships. However, this data is difficult to interpret because it is not apparent if personal adjustment leads to a higher likelihood of cohabitation or that cohabitation itself is likely to produce higher levels of personal adjustment.

Questions concerning plans for the future revealed strong agreement with the data

14

collected at Penn State. Neither cohabitors nor noncohabitors are rejecting the institution of marriage. In the Cornell study no sognificant difference was uncovered concerning future marriage plans for the two groups. Approximately 20 percent of the noncohabitors as well as the cohabitors indicated that they never planned to get married or that they did not feel marriage was necessary for future happiness.

Finally, the Cornell study asked the question of those who had not cohabited why they had not done so. Their answers give us some insight into the level of acceptance of cohabitation and the factor which are likely to lead to cohabitation. Over 50 percent of those who had not cohabited revealed that the reason they had not done so was "have not found someone with whom would like to stay for four or more nights a week" (26 percent) and "geographic distance from partner" (25 percent). Only 7 percent of the noncohabitors indicated that they considered cohabitation outside marriage morally wrong. It appears that many among those who are not cohabiting are not involved due to lack of opportunity rather than moral repugnance. What allows some to find and exercise this opportunity and others not is unclear, but certainly the great majority approve of the cohabitation life style during the college years.

Henze and Hudson (1974) at Arizona State University also analyzed some of the differences between cohabitors and noncohabitors. They report information on family and community background (type of home community, parental stability, education of parents, type of discipline, religion, church attendance), subjective evaluations of life style at present (conservative, middle of the road, liberal) and use of drugs. In comparing this data with that of the Penn State and Cornell studies, it sould be kept in mind that the rate of cohabitation among women was lower in this study than in either the Peterman, et al., or Macklin study, and that the male/female ratio is much closer at University of Arizona than either of the other institutions. Finally, there are the obvious geographic differences which are difficult to evaluate. However, all three campuses have similar housing regulations.

The researchers at Arizona State found more evidence of a double standard operating than had the researchers studying in the northeast. For example, they found a larger proportion of males with cohabitation experience than females, a larger percentage of the male cohabitors than female cohabitors had had more than one living-together relationship; and among those who were noncohabitors males indicated a greater interest in cohabitation than did females. Therefore, I will discuss the differences, indicated by the data, between cohabitors and noncohabitors by sex and then present the more general findings of the study.

Among the background variables employed, male cohabitors and noncohabitors could not be differentiated according to the type of area (urban, rural, suburban) in which they spent their childhood, parental education, type of discipline, or religion at birth. One of the variables which did differentiate male cohabitors from noncohabitors was family stability. Male cohabitors were more likely (approximately 30 percent) to have come from backgrounds in which divorce had taken place than were noncohabitors (less than 10 percent). Other variables on which the two groups could be differentiated included church attendance, evaluation of personal life style and use of drugs. Male cohabitors were less likely than noncohabitors to attend religious services once a month or more (11 percent and 39 percent respectively). They were more likely to classify themselves as having a liberal life style (63 percent) as opposed to the noncohabitors (22 percent). Finally, they were more likely to have used marijuana and hard drugs than the noncohabitors. The data indicates that 100 percent of the cohabitors had used marijuana, but less than 60 percent of the noncohabitors had done so. They were also 8 times more likely to have ever used hard drugs than noncohabitors, the percentages being 42 percent for cohabitors but only 5 percent for the noncohabitors.

The data presented by Henze and Hudson reveal that some variables which did not correlate with tendency to cohabit among males did correlate with female cohabitation. For females, the background variables of childhood setting, marital stability, or parental education did not differentiate between cohabitors and noncohabitors. However, type of dsicipline and religion at birth did show a correlation with cohabitation experience. The data reveals that female cohabitors were more likely than noncohabitors to come from backgrounds in which they evaluated parental discipline as strict. Fifty percent of the female cohabitors, but only 31 percent of the noncohabitors, classified the type of discipline in the home as restrictive. In terms of religious backgrounds, although Protestant accounted for over 60 percent of the noncohabitors, they were only 21 percent of those females who had cohabited. On the other hand, Catholic females, only 13 percent of the noncohabitors, accounted for nearly 30 percent of those females who did have living-together experience. The Arizona research, in agreement with the data at Penn State, found an overrepresentation of Catholic females from restrictive backgrounds. This finding suggests that those women who are subject to stricter discipline in the home and religious background are more likely to react to the vastly increased freedom of the college campus by experimenting with new patterns of behavior.

In the areas of church attendance, perception of life style and drugs, female cohabitors compared with noncohabitors in much the same way as we found among males. Interestingly the difference between female cohabitors and those without cohabitation experience is even more pronounced than for the two male groups in the areas of church attendance and life style. Nearly 40 percent of the female noncohabitors reported attending church once a month or more, but none of the cohabiting females reported this level of church attendance. Seventy-nine percent of the cohabiting females labeled their life style as liberal, but only 25 percent of the noncohabiting females classified themselves in this category. Finally, although here the differences were not as great as in the male group, female cohabitors were more likely to have ever used marijuana and hard drugs than the noncohabiting females.

Essentially, the major areas related to tendency to cohabit in the Arizona study are low church attendance, evaluation of life style as liberal, and higher levels of drug usage. Family background and characteristics did not appear to distinguish between cohabitors and noncohabitors although the combination of Catholic background and strict family discipline for remales, according to this data, may produce a reaction formation in the nonrestrictive college setting in which peers rather than parents set the standards.

Arafat and Yorburg (1973) attempted to distinguish between cohabiting and non-cohabiting students at City College in New York in their research conducted in 1971. Along with basic demographic data they included questions concerning influence of parents, peers and the mass media, willingness to engage in a living-together relationship and self-evaluation including level of independence and aggressiveness. Although only one-fifth of the students in their sample indicated experience in a living-together relationship, nearly 80 percent revealed that they would be willing to engage in cohabitation if given the opportunity to do so. In line with other researchers they found a strong relationship between religiosity and negative attitudes toward cohabitation. They did not, however, find the relationship between field of study and tendency to cohabit and suggest that it is the college student milieu rather than the particular field of study which effectively determines attitudes of behavior in this area. They also noted the lack of relationship between tendency to cohabit and social class origins.

An area in which the City College study was able to differentiate between those with living-together experience and those who had not cohabited was in self-image of the respondent. Three-quarters of the cohabitors, male and female, characterized themselves as independent, outgoing and aggressive; however, among the noncohabitors only 60 percent of the males and 58 percent of the females evaluated themselves in this way. As an aspect of this independence, the researchers noted that males and females involved in cohabitation were less likely to feel influenced by parents, peers or mass media than were noncohabitors. Given the opportunity to classify the degree of influence as great, moderate, or little, 63 percent of the male cohabitors described the degree of parental influence at "little," but only 43 percent of the male noncohabitors indicated this low degree of parental influence. For the female group the difference is even more striking; 60 percent of the female cohabitors indicated little parental influence, while 27 percent of the noncohabitors said their parents had this low a degree of influence on them.

Conclusion

A number of researchers have attempted to document the dvidence of cohabitation on the college campus and to differentiate between those students who are likely to cohabit as opposed to those who do not. Although certainly more study needs to be done, we have found that cohabitation is generally considered acceptable behavior by college students and that living together is becoming more and more a part of the college experience. Students who have not had cohabitation experience are open to this arrangement and often expect or want to become involved in a living-together arrangement. Although students at the various campuses studied had somewhat different views as to the type of relationship necessary before starting to live together, it is apparent that the great majority view premarital cohabitation as acceptable and increasingly expected behavior.

It is also clear that those who do cohabit are not dramatically different than those who do not. Although researchers have pointed out that cohabitors are less likely to hold strong religious beliefs, more likely to be enrolled in humanities curriculum, and somewhat more likely to evaluate themselves as independent and well adjusted, it seems that those students having cohabitation experience are quite similar to the general student population with cohabitation experience more a function of opportunity than demographic characteristics.

In sum, it appears then that we are dealing with a phenomenon increasingly becoming a part of the taken-for-granted life style of the contemporary college student.

CHAPTER II

RESEARCH METHODOLOGY

Research Design

A major problem in designing the research was that there was very little basis on which to build the empirical examination or a theoretical perspective. In what manner should the examination proceed? How should the research tools be organized? What considerations should be employed in selecting a sample? The subject I was interested in studying involved private, sensitive and, in fact, illegal behavior. There was no means of obtaining an accurate list of cohabitors. There was no solid theoretical basis on which to attack the problem. There was no previous scientific study to be criticized and reformulated.

The central concern of the research was to develop an understanding and realistic description of unmarried heterosexual cohabitation. The focus, moreover, of the research was to be directed toward the young middle class, well educated group which had been the primary target of both the popular literature and the scarce professional examination of this topic. In order to achieve this understanding it would be necessary to examine in detail both the backgrounds and the present realities of those participating in cohabitation relationships. To develop a means of uncovering the structure, expectations and responsibilities of the cohabiting couple, a broad range of questions concerning both attitudes and behavior had to be asked.

As I sought a basis for what I hoped to achieve in this sociological examination, a passage from Blumer's "Methodological Principles of Empirical Science" seemed particularly appropriate.

Exploratory study of human group life is the means of achieving simultaneously two complementary and interknit objectives. On the one hand, it is the way by which a research scholar can form a close and comprehensive acquaintance with a sphere of social life that is unfamiliar and hence unknown to him. On the other hand, it is a means of developing and sharpening his inquiry so that his problem, his directions of inquiry, data, analytical relations, and interpretations arise out of, and remain grounded in, the empirical life under study. (Blumer, 1969:32)

He goes on to state that:

The purpose of exploratory investigation is to move toward a clearer understanding of how one's problem is to be posed, to learn what are the appropriate data, to develop ideas of what are significant lines of relation, and to involve one's conceptual tools in the light of what one is learning about the area of life. In this respect it differs from the somewhat pretentious posture of the research scholar who under established scientific protocol is required in advance of his study to present a fixed and clearly structured problem, to know what kinds of data he is to collect, to have and hold to a prearranged set of techniques, and to shape his findings by previously established categories....All too frequently, the scholar confronted with an unfamiliar area of social life will fabricate, in advance, analytical schemes that he believes necessary to account for the problematic features of an area. One of the interesting values of exploratory study is that the fuller descriptive account that it yields will frequently give an adequate explanation of what was problematic without the need of involving any theory or proposing any analytical scheme. (Blumer, 1969:34)

Blumer explains that exploratory studies are not wedded to any particular set of techniques. He infers that researchers use any ethically viable procedures that offer potential for obtaining a clearer picture of what is actually going on in that area of social life. However, he does suggest that direct observation, interviewing and questioning, securing life histories and arranging group discussions are techniques that are extremely worthwhile in such exploratory research.

In this research concerned with an area of social life, heretofore not attacked in the sociological literature, the advantages of an exploratory design are directly applicable. In adapting the various techniques suggested by Blumer to the study of unmarried heterosexual cohabitation, the establishment of a concrete empirical base is appropriate. As Selltiz, et al., also points out, the purpose of this dissertation is consistent with the goals of an exploratory study. As they suggest:

> The relative youth of social science and the scarcity of social science research make it inevitable that much of this research, for a time to come will be of this pioneering character. Few well-trodden paths exist for the investigator of social relations to follow; theory is often too general or too specific to provide clear guidance for empirical research. In these circumstances, exploratory research is necessary to obtain the experience that will be helpful in formulating relevant hypotheses for more definitive investigation. (Selltiz, et al., 1959:51-52)

In Selltiz's explanation of this type of study she points out that three basic methods are most appropriate in conducting exploratory research: "(1) a review of the related social science and other pertinent literature; (2) a survey of people who have had practical experience with the problem to be studied; and (3) an analysis of 'insight stimulating' examples." (Selltiz, et al., 1959:53)

The experience survey as defined by Selltiz, et al., suggests interviewing specialists who have "a reservoir of experience" in dealing with the area under study. However, since the growth of this phenomenon took place in such a short period of time there did not, as yet, exist a knowledgeable group of potential respondents who were capable of providing the level of information I was seeking. Selltiz, et al., make it clear that, "In an experience survey it is a waste of time and effort to interview people who have little competence, or little relevant experience, or who lack ability to communicate their experience." (Selltiz, et al., 1959:56)

The final method suggested by Selltiz, et al., the examination of insight stimulating examples, seemed most appropriate to the purposes of my study. "Scientists working in relatively unformulated areas, where there is little experience to serve as a guide, have found the intensive study of selected examples to be a particularly fruitful method for stimulating insights and suggesting hypothesis for research." They suggest, as Blumer does, that the use of questioning, interviewing, and observation are the most appropriate means of detailing the intensive examination of examples of the phenomenon in which one is interested.

In the remainder of this chapter I will outline the means by which the empirical data was gathered, provide a description of the research tools, and specifically describe the manner in which the tools and the method were applied.

The Sample

The major purpose of the study demanded that I collect a great deal of information from my respondents. In choosing the sample population to be studied I was less interested in gaining a necessarily representative sample than I was in obtaining a sample that would be accessible "(a sample selected on the basis of convenience is sometimes called a 'chunk')" (Riley, 1963:296) and small enough to permit intensive analysis. As Riley points out, "Such loosely defined samples are frequently useful in exploratory studies." (Riley, 1963:296) A relevant problem in a study of this sort is the lack of access to the universe of the conceptual model. I determined that I would select 50 couples on which to gather data. Furthermore, that I would restrict the sample to those cohabiting couples in which each considered their primary residence to be the one in which they cohabited and, finally, that they themselves defined their situation as a cohabiting relationship.

The methodology employed in obtaining the respondents would not qualify the sample as either random or representative. A random sample in which every member (couple) of the universe (of heterosexual consensual unions) stands an equal change of being included was both impractical and unnecessary for my purposes. A simple random sample is only possible in a situation in which the universe of the population is known. Since there is no cnesus listing of unmarried couples, and since at least some of these couples attempt to conceal the fact that they are unmarried, a truly random sample would be impossible. In fact, the sample consisted of respondents gathered from a "snowball sample" procedure: i.e., first interviewing a small sample of people, asking these people who their friends are, interviewing these friends and so on. James Coleman (1959:32) points out that the sampling then follows the sociometric relationships of the universe.

In this study of living-together couples, the snowball procedure also provides data which can be helpful in evaluating the social relationship which these couples maintain. Who are their friends? How many couples do they know who are participating in similar life styles. Furthermore, speculation concerning the level of social reinforcement, which they may have or seek can be made.

The sample was drawn from the population of undergraduate and graduate students from the various campuses of Rutgers University in and around New Brunswick, New Jersey. Though most respondents were students, even those who were not officially connected with the university were well integrated into the academic atmosphere of the college campus.*

The Research Instruments

Questionnaire (see Appendix I)

The questionnaire provides a means of obtaining a wide range of information from respondents which would have been more difficult to categorize and more time consuming in an interview situation. The questionnaire, due to its standardized wording, order of questions, and instructions for recording responses, ensures some uniformity from one measurement situation to another. Although there is always the problem of the same wording having diverse meanings for different people, careful pretesting and providing help during its administration can ensure meaningful uniformity.

One aim of the research was to gather some very basic initial data about those young people involved in cohabitation relationships. An extensive questionnaire was developed and pretested on a small sample of unmarried couples. The questionnaire covered a wide range of subjects including background information (age, religion, politics, etc.), the development of the relationship, its present state, and its probable future. The questionnaire posed a wide range of attitudinal questions that dealt with such issues as abortion, political reform, drug usage, sexual morality, renewable marriages, church attendance, parental reactions, family life, divorce,

_____

*As an aside it might be noted that one couple referred me to a homosexual couple who had been living together but were unmarried. A decision was made to carry out the research including having them fill out the questionnaires and complete the interview. Although the information gained was not included in the analysis here, I did find the questionnaire and the structured interview to be perfectly adaptable to the homosexual couple.

and women's liberation. I also called forth information that helps to explicitly define the structure, the expectations and the responsibilities of the heterosexual consensual union. It included questions concerning: the type of community in which respondents lived; how long they had been living together; whether they had a history of experimentation with alternative life types; as well as questions concerning their attitudes toward traditional marriage, personal privacy and respect for parents.

Along with the above mentioned attitudinal questions the questionnaire posed inquiries aimed at evaluating or describing actual behavior. Who pays the rent? Who washes the dishes? How do they describe their relationship? What difficulties or areas of disagreement have they encountered? How do they (individually and together) spend their leisure time? Do they take separate vacations? etc.

The questionnaire, though basic, was only one part of the research design. Also included were structured and unstructured interviews, group discussions with a number of cohabiting couples and participant observation.

The Interview (see Appendix II)

Selltiz, et al., point out that although the questionnaire and interview are both forms of questioning, the interview does provide some unique possibilities for obtaining information.

"Although both interviews and questionnaires place heavy reliance upon the validity of verbal reports, there are important differences between the two methods. In a questionnaire the information one obtains is limited to the writter response of subjects to prearranged questions. In an interview, since the interviewer and the person interviewed are both present as the questions are asked and answered, there is opportunity for greater flexibility in eliciting information; in addition the interviewer has the opportunity to observe both the subject and the total situation to which he is responding." (Selltiz, et al., 1959:238).

The interview situation, therefore, has the advantage of being flexible, allows the interviewer to observe not only what the respondent says but how he says it, and provides a means of following up on contradictory statements. Certainly, on more complex questions where there may be strong emotional involvement--as, for example, questions of sexual fidelity or the future of the relationship--the interviewer is likely to be more successful in revealing information than is the more rigid questionnaire. Particularly applicable to this study, as Selltiz, et al., point out: "The more or less rigid structure of questionnaires, the inability to explain fully in writing one's asocial or antisocial feelings and behavior, and the solemnity and permanent nature of a response that is put on paper in one's own handwriting or (if the questionnaire is not anonymous) as in this case under one's own name - all work against frank discussions of socially taboo or socially controversial issues in response to a questionnaire. With respect to many questions, an interview is likely to be more successful in creating an atmosphere that allows the respondent to express feelings or to report behaviors that are customarily disapproved." (Selltiz, et al., 1959:242-243)

The partially structured interview was a necessity in this study so that I would have the opportunity to explore the attitudes, perceptions and motivations of my respondents. They were freer to admit certain feelings and behavior in the individual interview situation than to write it down on the questionnaire form. The flexibility helped to bring out the effective and value laden aspects of the subject's responses. This flexibility is both an advantage and a disadvantage: it offers greater exploratory potential yet limits the comparability with other interviews. In an exploratory study of this nature, however, the advantages far outweigh the disadvantages in terms of achieving greater understanding.

One purpose of the partially structured interview was to examine in greater detail the information gathered in the questionnaire. Where the questionnaire focused to a large extent on background information, the interview focused on the manner in which the cohabiting relationship had evolved. The verbal exchange between the researcher and the respondent allowed the opportunity to clarify the present situation as well as to explore the respondents feelings and attitudes toward the future of the relationship.

Importantly, the face-to-face contact between researcher and respondent also provided an opportunity to check the reliability and the validity of the information gathered by means of the questionnaire. In each case, as will be further explained below, each member of the couple was interviewed individually and then they were interviewed together.

The interview was only partially structured and certainly not limited to the questions in the interview schedule. In as much as this was an exploratory study, whenever areas of interest came up in the interview they were pursued in order to increase the researcher's understanding and to explore new areas of inquiry.

Group Discussions

On several occasions the opportunity arose to interview or discuss cohabitation with a group of cohabitors. Sometimes the situation arose without formal planning (flexibility), in other cases I had formally arranged a time and place for a number of cohabiting couples to gather and discuss various aspects of unmarried hetero-sexual cohabitation. On two occasions, while I was interviewing a cohabiting couple, they were visited by another cohabiting couple and I did not pass up the opportunity for all of us to get involved in a group interview situation. On one occasion, after completing an interview with one couple, they invited two other couples, who were also cohabiting, to join us and continue our examination of these relationships. Though these discussions were rather unstructured, they did provide interesting insights particularly with respect to the range of orientations toward living together that respondents felt. In fact, toward the end of the study the group discussions were extremely helpful in developing the typology of unmarried cohabitation presented in Chapter 3 of this study.

Observation

Here I am using the term observation in a rather general sense and I should explain the exact manner in which this observation took place. Interviews in all but one case took place in the home of the respondents, and in quite a few cases the researcher was invited to stay for dinner, drinks or merely to continue interesting discussion on an informal basis. Interviewing respondents in their own home not only made them more confortable and at ease, but that situation allowed for the observation of respondents interaction in its usual setting, the manner in which household chores were divided, and the amount or level of material conforts in their homes. Information such as who answered the phone, who served coffee and how the couple interacted with others became accessible. Often it was possible to observe the couple's interaction with friends, landlords and even parents. Although this type of observation could hardly be termed systematic, it did provide, as with the group discussions, some unique opportunities to develop clearer understandings about the subject matter under scrutiny.

It should be made clear that not all respondents participated in group discussions, and that more time was spent with some couples than with others. Interviews lasted approximately two and one-half to three hours (a few were shorter, others much longer). In some cases the same couple was seen a number of times; and, in a few cases, friendships developed which led to continued informal interaction between the researcher and respondents.

Data Collection Procedure

The two major research tools were the questionnaire and the interview. Both dealt with the individual level and the dyadic or couple level. The actual procedure can be outline briefly as follows: I would arrange with the couple a time convenient to them when they would be willing to spend approximately three hours together with the researcher. In most cases interviews started just after dinner, although a few of the interviews did take place during the day. After a short explanation of the research one partner would take the questionnaire to another part of the house and fill it out while the interview with the other partner took place.* They would then change places and a second individual interview would be completed. Finally, the couple together would be interviewed and points of clarification would be offered where the two parties had made somewhat conflicting statements. As an example, if Alice said her relationship with her parents was the same as before she started "living together" while Bill (her partner disagreed, we would discuss and clarify in what way the relationship had changed or remained the same. In this three-part interview a high degree of informational reliability was achieved. The separate interview served as a means of discovering both actual facts and inconsistencies. At times it also served as an informal attitude revealing device, e.g., in the interview with Loretta and Gordon:

Individual Interview - Gordon

Researcher: Do you have any formal or informal agreements about sexual fidelity?

Gordon: We agreed early in the game that either of us can go out with whoever we want whenever we want to.

Researcher: Do you or Loretta actually go out with other people?

Gordon: Each of us has a few times but not lately. I guess neither of us wants to go out with anyone else right now. But we haven't set up any rules against it.

Individual Interview - Loretta

Researcher: Do you have any formal or informal agreements about sexual fidelity?

Loretta: When we first started living together we said that we wouldn't stop each other from seeing other people. Gordon went out a few times with an old girl friend of his and I didn't like it. But when I wanted to go out and did, he would not officially say no but he would be very bitchy when I got back. I decided if we were going to live together I just better not see other people.

Researcher: Did you and Gordon discuss the situation and decide on a monogamous relationship?

Loretta: Not really; we just didn't do it anymore.

---

*As Riley, et al., (1963:189), warn: "There is clearly a danger of control effect if one member, who has already been questioned, discusses the matter with another member who has not yet been questioned. The researcher may offset this effect by one of the following devices: by using several interviewers in order to question all the group members simultaneous; in a two member group, such as husband and wife, by conducting one interview immediately after the other without allowing any interim interaction between the two members; or by administering a written questionnaire to all members at the same time.

In the interview with the couple it became obvious that the matter was still to some extent unresolved, although Gordon's perception of the process was somewhat different thatn Loretta's. The end product of exclusivity apparently developed from a fear of loss rather than from a positive decision not to be involved in outside relationships.

The purpose of the separate interview was twofold: First, to give privacy to the individual respondent; and, secondly, to develop a means of obtaining reliability and validity of responses. In some cases the respondent revealed in the individual interviews attitudes or infidelities that he/she was not sharing with his/her partner. In a few cases I found differences in attitudes expressed privately (i.e., individual interview) and as a couple. Occasionally it became apparent that respondents were more concerned about sexual fideltiy or marriage, for example, than they would openly display in front of their partner.

Generally I found that open communication between the partners was an important concern. Though there were examples of partners keeping secrets from each other, more often it was the subtle differences in perception of the relationship that could be uncovered with this method. In fact, in most cases I found respondents extremely open and apparently honest about their relationships, past experiences and future plans.

The sample reported here consists of 50 couples. A computer program was developed to print out the responses as a couple and as individuals. This by no means reflects the total amount of information obtained during the period of research. I spoke with some young poeple who had lived together but were no longer involved in a "living-together" relationship. I spoke to a number of couples who had cohabited but were presently married. Furthermore, two couples were willing to be interviewed but would not fill out questionnaires, maintaining that to categorize their relationship would not do it justice, and they did not want to be part of a sociologist's classification of their existence. (These couples were not part of the sample reported.)

In summary, I focused on two levels, the individual and the dyad (couple). I was interested in an exploratory study and chose an analytic sample which would represent predominantly middle class college age and recent college graduate young people involved in unmarried heterosexual cohabitation. I sought information about their past, present and future, attempted to ask questions from a variety of viewpoints and to avoid making value judgements about their behavior. I employed a questionnaire, interviews and observation to gather the data for the study, and I plan to present both systematic findings (i.e., percentages, classification, etc.) and descriptive analysis. I received a high degree of cooperation from respondents who found many of the questions interesting and revealing. The group discussions ran from the creation of utopian communities to the analyzation of the value of renewable marriages.

Although a scientifically chosen sample was not obtained, the central concern was to develop an understanding and realistic picture of the unmarried heterosexual cohabiting couple. I believe I was successful in achieving that goal.

CHAPTER III

FACTORS GENERATING INCREASED EXPERIMENTATION WITH
UNMARRIED HETEROSEXUAL COHABITATION

This chapter presents the major factors which helped to create an atmosphere in which increased adaptation of a life style including unmarried cohabitation became possible among, educated, middle class people in the late 1960's and early 1970's. Each of these factors has had a two-fold effect in that each played a part in increasing the opportunity for such relationships at the same time as they decreased social controls which censured or prohibited this type of behavior. Furthermore, it is clear that although some of these conditions have existed over a period of time, the convergence of social factors and events which occurred during the 1960's gave significant impetus to a trend which probably would have appeared at a later date in any case.

As Yankelovich (1974:1) has pointed out in his study of youth values:
The 1960's were characterized by many unique events....The short but vivid era of the Kennedy presidency, the rise of the Civil Rights Movement under the leadership of Martin Luther King, the abrupt impact of the inner city riots and burnings swiftly followed by the student riots on campus, the shock of the assasinations of John and Robert Kennedy and Martin Luther King--all these events certainly left their mark on the times. The one event which these findings suggest most strongly influenced the values and views of a generation was, of course, the Vietnam War. It is possible to see, now, in retrospect, that the spirit of political radicalism on campus was inextricably interrelated with student response to the war in Southeast Asia. The draft forged an intensely personal link between the students and a far off war which inspired loathing, fear and revulsion on campus. The small core of political radicals, never more than 10-15 percent of the college population, took the lead in interpreting the war in terms that were harshly critical of the United States, its motives, its institutions and its moral impulses. Because they were so disturbed by the war, the great mass of college students accepted the radical critique and, especially in the Ivy League colleges, joined the New Left in its attack on the universities and other institutions that were interpreted as being part of the web of immorality and misuse of power that students associated with the war. Inevitable, Vietnam-inspired political radicalism became entangled with the cluster of new life styles and social values that had their genesis in an earlier period.

I have provided this long quote from the Yankelovich study because his continuous research of the country's youth population allows him the advantage of incorporating and comparing findings with his earlier studies. Moreover, this quotation briefly summarizes the historical setting of the 1960's and sets the stage for the analysis of social factors related to changing patterns of cohabitation among the young, educated population in which I was interested.

It is important that Yankelovich concludes that though there were many unique aspects to the 1960's and early 70's, young people are not returning to the status quo of the 1950's. He states that the war represented an aberration from the mainstream of American social history and that youthful values intimately tied to the war and the strong emotions it evoked came and went with the war. However, in answer to the question as to whether we are picking up the threads of cultural continuity where we left off in the 1950's, these national surveys indicate that nothing could be further from the truth.

Analyzing the data collected in 1971-72 for the John D. Rockefeller III Fund and the Task Force on Youth, which concentrated on college youth, Yankelovich (1972:7) concluded that:

Radical political values and life styles which traveled together since the mid 1960's have in 1971 begun to go their separate ways. Changing cultural values--relationships to marriage, authority, religion, work, money, career, sexual morality, and other aspects of the puritan ethic--have become more marked and dramatic each year since these measurements began (1967), including 1971....The vast majority of students--have pressed forward in their search for a cultural revolution while taking a step backward from political revolution.

And from his later studies:

The war was vivid and traumatic while it lasted, but the enduring heritage of the 1960's is the new social values that grew on the nation's campuses during the same fateful period and now have grown stronger and more powerful. (Yankelovich, 1974:12)

In the following sections I examine the economic socio-cultural and technological factors including: rejection of established values (alienation and intergenerational conflict); expanding demand for an opportunity for higher education; middle class affluence; liberation movements; changing sexual mores and technological advances as well as increasing divorce rates which converged during this time period to produce an environmental setting in which unmarried heterosexual cohabitation would become possible, desirable, even socially acceptable.

Rejection of the Establishment

Intergenerational conflict is by no means a recent phenomenon. The ancient Greeks complained about the lack of obedience of youth. However, the rebellion of young people in the United States had never been as great as it was in the mid 1960's and early 1970's. In fact, many of these young people had gone beyond rebellion. Some dismissed the entire society as sick, immoral or unlivable. (Bell, 1971:50; Keniston, 1965, 1971; Flacks, 1971) That generation, however, was not passive or withdrawing. They participated, confronted, demonstrated, protested, and at times destroyed. They turned on, dropped out, and sought to build alternatives. Flacks traces the emergence of the yough movements of the late 60's to its beginnings among certain college students of the 1950's. He suggests that these "intellectual youths" were the forerunners and that "over the course of the subsequent decade the initially mild cultural criticism articulated by young intellectuals became increasingly political, radical, and rebellious." (Flacks, 1971:60) Among the young people who were influenced by the beatnick movement of the 1950's and the civil rights movement of the 1960's was a small group that organized the protest over the war in Viet Nam. They led the protest for student rights and were responsible for the demonstrations which received intensive news media interest and coverage of these events.

Although the alination began in the political sphere, it soon spread to other aspects of American life. Social institutions and mores such as marriage, the family, and sexual behavior were subjected to critical re-evaluation. Many started to reconsider the values and goals by which they had been raised. It has been taken for granted that part of becoming an adult involves getting married and having children. Monogamy has been viewed as the natural living state of normal adult members of the society. The female of our species has been socialized into roles that are clearly wife and mother oriented. During this period, however, some students began to question the viability and necessity of marriage, the practicality or desirability of having children, and the seeming unrealistic and unnecessary confinement of mono-gamous marriage. These protesting, experimenting students were symptomatic of a society that was experiencing certain forces and phenomena that might produce varia-tion in or even the disappearance of traditional aspects of becoming a "grownup" in contemporary America. Much of the energy that had been channeled into the political sphere in the late 1960's was apparently being channeled inwardly into personal experiments by the early 1970's. The alienation which produced a rejection of the established system and traditional roles simultaneously opened the door to exper-imentation with new forms and less rigidly prescribed rules of conduct.

It was clear that many students came to believe that "the system" did not work any more. Loss of faith in the 1960's may be seen as a consequence of occurrences both on and off the campus. The Vietnam War, the civil rights movement, the credi-bility gap, etc., all played their part in creating in the minds of students a pic-ture of an established system that didn't refelct their needs or their desires. More-over, they believe the "system" apparently neither worked effectively nor dealt honestly with their segment of the constituency. Student leaders who fought in these causes were presented with a large number of issues on which to attack the estab-lishment, the authority structure and the values that supported that structure. Controls formerly accepted now represented an encroachment on the freedom of the individual. Those who fought for black civil rights or against the war also demanded students' rights and privileges. The value structure, the norms, the goals of the society were being questioned. Perhaps we can more clearly grasp what occurred by understanding that there is a profound difference between someone who breaks the rules and someone who does not accept the rules. Whether we think in terms of at-titudes toward authority or sexual behavior, we find young people during this period not just breaking the rules but considering rules invalid. Those representing or standing behind those rules, behind a society that did not live up to its ideals, were in many ways rejected also.

During this period of protest students felt an obligation to exercise their right to reform the social codes which seemed to unreasonably limit their behavior. The strains generated by these conflicts resulted in the allowance of greater re-sponsibility and freedom for youth.

The College Experience

Importantly, the protest movements, the demonstrations, the anti-establishment attitudes developed and were acted out in a setting most often confined to the college campus. In our examination of cohabitation it is necessary to review the changes taking place on the college campus which affected the environmental opportunity for unmarried heterosexual cohabitation.

The college experience had become increasingly accessible to a wide range of the youthful population. During the decade of the 1960's the college population doubled from three and one-half million to seven million. Furthermore, the fact that in-creasing numbers of young people were being brought together, in an age segregated setting, enhanced their feelings of peer group identification. Since the college student is nearly completely immersed in that culture, it is the members of that culture which provide the recognition, the status, and the approval for his actions and behavior. If the college student population reflects, in general, the attitudes deemed acceptable in the society, this segregation is not nearly as significant as when the student population is in the process of rejecting what has been viewed as appropriate by the larger society. This segregation then has a more dramatic effect in enhancing group solidarity and identification when students are alienated from the mainstream. In the 1960's we saw a more distinct differentiation between "campus values" and that of the larger society than we had ever experienced in our institutions of higher education. Furthermore, there was a significant decrease in the level of control over the lives of college students during the latter 1960's. In the past much of parental authority was transferred to the college administrator when one traded the confinement of the parental domicile for that of the college dormitory. College students had been subject to rules and regulations which included a wide variety of restrictions on their freedom. To some extent men, but particularly college women, lived in sex segregated dormitories complete with curfew times, restrictions against visits from members of the opposite sex as well as strict requirements against stay- ing out overnight. Certainly these restrictions were on almost every campus more limiting and carefully enforced for women than for men.

Since this dissertation is concerned with a sample of cohabitants drawn from the Rutgers University community (many are now college students or recent graduates), an examination of the changing residential requirements and regulations on the Rutgers and Douglass campuses can be illustrative. Interviews with administrators and residence counselors reveal that certainly attitudes and regulations have changed and that the setting clearly provided greater potential for cohabiting relationships in the early 1970's than in the dark ages of 1965. On both the Rutgers and Douglass campuses these changes began in the later 60's.

At Douglass College my interview with the director of residence revealed that the administration saw the need and began attempting to have regulations be more congruent with changing attitudes. Students in the late 60's were, in fact, often breaking the curfew rules and allowing visitors to remain in restricted areas after visiting hours. The shift from very tight regulations to aomost no restrictions took place in a rather short time. In the mid 60's all Douglass dormitories had strict curfews and violations resulted in appearance before a judicial committee. Each girl had to ask and receive permission to sign out overnight, and parental as well as college adminis- trative consent was necessary. A few quotations from the Douglass College student handbook (1964-65) indicate the level of in loco parentis at that time.

"Signing IN AND OUT -
A. The student must sign out on her card in her dorm when she is going to be absent from the house after 7:00 p.m. Her sign-out should indicate where she expects to spend the major part of the evening. If the destination is changed after leaving campus, the student should call the dormitory and have her sign-out changed accordingly.

B. She must sign out any time she leaves the City of New Brunswick.

C. She must sign in immediately upon return.

"Curfew
A. Callers may be entertained on the resident campuses during the hours specified by the respective campus governments.

B. Male relatives emphasis mine may be entertained in the dormi- tory rooms on Sunday afternoons 2:00 - 5:45.

    (A student entertaining a gentleman caller at an unauthorized time should be asked to report herself.)"

These regulations perpetuated a high level of social control over the lives of Douglass students. They had to sign in and out during evening hours, there were strict curfews, and no male visitors were allowed in dorm rooms except relatives, and even then restricted to Sunday afternoons. The first change was to extend curfews, then increased visiting, and finally to abolish the curfew entirely and extend visita- tion to 24 hours. By the early 1970's regulations or restrictions of any kind had been almost eliminated. No curfew, 24-hour visitation for any guest, optional sign-out sheets, and no need for either parental or adminstrative approval for staying out overnight. In terms of cohabitation the director of residence at Douglass explained, "We stress visitation and we are opposed to cohabitation in the dormitories. This can be offensive to other women, and when complaints are made we do something about it." She explained further that all the changes in these regulations came through student demands, but no real protest or demonstrations took place. Administrators attempted to study the issue, and a committee was formed which eventually went along with student desires. The director explained further that not all women desired dorms with 24-hour visitation, and that fifteen percent of the women still reside in dorms which have restrictive visiting hours, but no students were subject to curfew regulations.

A similar pattern can be found at Rutgers; however, since there were, in fact, less restrictions at Rutgers the transition was quicker than at Douglass. Male students were not subject to curfews, did not have sign-out sheets, and did not need permission to stay out overnight. The only real change was the formal approval of allowing female visitors to the dorm and then extending that privilege to a 24-hour basis. (In the sample that I reported, two of the respondents were residence counselors who were involved in nonmarital cohabitation.)

Macklin also suggests a relationship between changes in dormitory regulations and the experience of cohabitation. After examining the changes in regulations at Cornell (very similar to those at Rutgets and Douglass) Macklin summarized by stating

One cannot consider the above changes in curfew and dorm policy to be primarily responsible for the cohabitation pattern which has evolved. These changes in policy are but a reflection of broader social changes: a change in the perception of women which now makes it hard to justify having different regulations for men and for women; a movement to grant individuals greater opportunity to determine their own life styles; youth's increasing demand that they no longer be treated as children; and so forth. However, it does seem reasonable to assume that changes in the regulations have facilitated changes in behavior, and the increase in the incidence of cohabitation seems clearly related to the relaxation of dormitory policy. (Macklin, 1971:3)

Interviews with respondents in this sample also strongly supported the concept that college meant an opportunity to be released from more restrictive moral codes. In response to the question, "Has college changed your moral values?" many indicated that the freedom they experienced in college allowed them to adopt new standards. According to many respondents, perceived societal norms no longer restricted their behavior. For example, a typical comment made by one female respondent was, "Before entering college I felt myself to be very much tied to society's norms; I now consider morals to be only what the individual decides, and I no longer adhere to those set down by society." Another stated, "Now that I am on my own away from parents and my home town I have gotten away from the puritan values I once held." Others mentioned that they weren't sure if it was the college experience of just "growing up" and being on their own. In either case it was clear that many felt the independence of college life allowed them to reconsider formerly held norms and standards in a setting that was extremely liberal in terms of sexual mores.

Middle Class Affluence

Middle and upper-middle class youth in the late 1960's and early 1970's had not only the time but the affluence that permitted them to seek a variety of experience. Whitehurst points out the connection between middle class affluence and the increase in cohabitation.

Due principally to high levels of affluence youth have been given
freedom to experiment, to exercise more varieties of psychosocial
moratoria. The shift to more LTU living together unmarried behaviour
has been most pronounced in the middle classes where affluence has
made the most difference in life style potentials....Accompanying
the increased affluence and sense of freedom to experiment has been
a general weakening of the societal controls over sexual (and other)
behaviour. When youth more frequently are sent away to university,
have their own automobiles and living places, families as the prin-
cipal source of sexual sanction lose power. (Whitehurst, 1973:3)

Perhaps since these young people experienced this affluence and material well-being since childhood, an occupational role and the material rewards it might offer were not as enticing as they once were. (Yankelovich, 1972, 1974) Furthermore, these students existed in a situation in which parents were often willing and able to provide funds so that their children could do "what they never could." Few young-sters of college age in the past had the freedom or the capital necessary for summers in Europe of travels around the United States. But the summers of the late 60's and early 70's produced a plethora of charter flights as well as individuals or couples wandering in search of good times, history, drugs and experiences. Im-portantly, these adventures took place almost exclusively within the world community of young people. The role of student often included travel and experience as well as study and football games. It is not merely the affluence that is important in this analysis, but the ever growing notion and reality that they were functioning extremely independently in all aspects of existence except perhaps their finances.

So in college, travel, in use of drugs, and through the attention of media, young people were being increasingly separated from the rest of society and the social controls of that society. But if we are to understand the implications for the college student, we must give consideration to other aspects of the social environment which were concurrently changing the atmosphere and potential for unmarried heterosexual cohabitation.

Sexual Revolution

An integral aspect of the environmental opportunity for unmarried heterosexual cohabitation is the changing attitudes and behavior patterns in sexual relationships. Although writers disagree as to whether there has been a "sexual revolution" in this country, it is clear that many of the alternative residential patterns experimented with in the late 1960's and early 1970's would not have been possible with formerly held norms of moral conduct. Unmarried heterosexual cohabitation is only possible in an atmosphere where premarital sex is not accompanied by overwhelming feelings of guilt. Though premarital sex among males has long been deemed acceptable, even desirable and necessary, female premarital sexual experience has only recently seen some positive reinforcement. In their observances on the college sexual scene Bell and Chashes' report that

the social forces developing since the mid 1960's have led to a rapid
increase in rejecting many traditional values and developing important
patterns of behavior common to a general youth culture. And out of this
has come an increased rate of premarital coitus among many college girls,

along with less feelings of guilt about their experiences. (Bell, 1971:52)

Ira Reiss, author of <u>The Social Context of Premarital Sexual Permissiveness</u>, argued in 1967 that the movement, at that time, toward permissiveness was within a greater context of general liberality. Reiss (1967:73) suggested that

....liberalism emphasizes the types of social forces that maintain high permissiveness for example, low religious orthodoxy, value on tradition, high value on autonomy. The stronger the amount of general liberality in a group, the greater likelihood that social forces will maintain high levels of sexual permissiveness.

Essentially this new moral code suggests two important consequences for the contemporary woman; the social value of feminine virginity is decreasing and the double standard, which tolerated sexual permissiveness for the male but demanded premarital virginity for the female, is no longer acceptable. As I noted in the study at Cornell, senior women who were virgins, although not obsolete, were clearly a small minority of the population. The decline of virginity is symptomatic of a changing value structure that allows for greater sexual experience and therefore eliminates an important barrier to the formation of the unmarried couple lifestyle.

Obviously the development, distribution and acceptance of "the pill" was also an important factor. On campuses across the country the pill became available to the coed, or not difficult for her to find in the local community. Technological advances such as the pill and increased use of other contraceptive devices allow for a greater amount of sexual freedom without fear and, according to Bell (1971:51), less guilt. Rather than merely focusing on the issue of increased sexual activity, I am suggesting that technology played a role in the area of sexual freedom and was another example of a barrier which was removed in setting the stage for future breakdowns in other traditions of the society.

My interviews reveal that these unmarried cohabitors depended on the pill and were confident about its effectiveness. Many of the women also indicated that the pill certainly did have an effect on their level of sexual interaction even before beginning a cohabitation relationship. They related that the security of knowing they were protected reduced, to some extent, the level of intensity of a relationship necessary before they would become involved in a sexually intimate encounter. Philip Houser (1969:35) in making predictions for the future of the family stated:

Premarital and extramarital sexual relationships will probably become increasingly acceptable in our society and be less hidden than in the past. Premarital relationships may increase greatly because of the established gap between age of sexual maturation and the provision of conventional opportunities for sexual gratification. They may increase, too, because of the greater availability of contraceptive devices and the attendant loss of fear about pregnancy.

The implication for unmarried heterosexual cohabitation is quite clear. Richard Farson (1969:63) in his evaluation of the future of the family suggests that "people will enjoy living together more, with or without marriage; and we shall see a great many such arrangements that do not invoke a legal contract. That is already happening."

Liberation Movements

Those staunch fighters for women's rights, civil rights, those against the war or for student rights were not necessarily the same individuals who were involved in unmarried heterosexual cohabitation. However, these movements and the positions taken by their leaders contributed to a situation and social atmosphere which helped set the stage on which this new life style of young people could be played.

Apparently the various liberation movements have also contributed to the increased potential for unmarried cohabitation. The Women's Liberation movement has been most influential, but other movements, such as Black Liberation, also had an effect. The message of these movements is that society constrains and exploits certain people. The recommended solution is to extract one's self from the traditional social grip. The liberationists are seeking emancipation from formerly prescribed rules of conduct. As Bell (1971:357) stated "...it is argued here that the movement Women's Liberation will not fade away and, in fact, quite possibly may become one of the most important social movements of the 1970's." What effect, if any, does this movement have on the potential for unmarried heterosexual cohabitation? One of the major attacks being made by the leaders in the movement is that the American family, with its primary socialization into "sexist" roles, is one of the main obstacles to women's equality. "All of the lib groups see the present conjugal family structure with its traditional division of labor as destructive to full female identity." (Bell, 1971:389) In fact some of the respondents stated quite clearly that they were attempting in their cohabiting relationship to avoid falling into the trap of sexist division of labor. (My findings indicate that they were not terribly successful in this area.) One might argue that feminists are unlikely candidates for heterosexual cohabiting relationships; yet it is clear that women rejecting the society's traditional marriage structure are more likely to experiment with alternative situations.

Rising Divorce Rates

Another factor which played some role in encouraging cohabitation was the increasing divorce rates. (Montgomery, 1973:330) In interviews respondents indicated that the increasing number of divorces that they were aware of forced them to question whether marriage was as viable an institution as it was "supposed" to be. In a few cases respondents pointed to specific instances of inadequate marriage situations either in their own family or among others that they knew. However, more often it was a general attitude about increasing divorce which developed from the media, and apparently respondents have an accurate interpretation of the situation. According to the U.S. Bureau of the Census, Statistical Abstract of the United States: 1972, the 1971 figure of 768,000 divorce decrees was the highest national total ever observed for the United States. These statistics further indicate that the number of divorces has been increasing more rapidly than the total population and the married population of the United States, and that since 1965 the divorce rate has been climbing relatively sharply. Importantly, whether respondents had indicated that their parents marriage was happy or not, they very nearly universally expressed the view that divorce was becoming more common.

Transadulthood

Many factors have been cited as contributing to an atmosphere which allowed for greater experimentation with unmarried heterosexual cohabitation including rejection of established values, the college experience, affluence, changing sexual standards, technological advances, women's liberation and an increasing divorce rate. However, it appears that much of what has occurred may be more clearly understood if we examine these factors within the framework of the emergence of a new stage in the life cycle which I have termed "transadulthood"(transition into adulthood). (Danziger and Greenwald, 1973)

It cannot be said that all cohabitors are transadults or that all transadults will become involved in cohabitation experiences. However, the essence of this analysis lies in the fact that the characteristics of individuals involved in this stage of life make them particularly adaptable to a life style which might include cohabitation.

In the section which follows I describe the stage of transadulthood in historical context and point out the characteristics of individuals who find themselves in this stage.

The process of becoming an adult has been found to be quite different in various cultures. In most traditional and "primitive" cultures this transition is rather straightforward. It often involves a rather definitive rite of passage and is a relatively simple "melting" into the adult role. Flacks, the author of Youth and Social Change, points out that in these societies one's adult identity is largely determined by the geographic and social location into which one is born. Therefore, one adopts a rather narrow definition of the adult role primarily through the model of parents and grandparents who transmit the culture. (Flacks, 1971:49)

Moore (1960:102) presents three criteria which appear to be basic to becoming an adult in most societies. They are:
1. Demonstrating that one has been educated and trained according to the expectations of the community, including a thorough indoctrination in the heritage of the society.

2. Proving oneself capable of defending the community and performing a trade or vocation.

3. Successful mating with a person of the opposite sex.

In modern or post-industrial societies (e.g., the United States), the transition to adulthood is a far more differentiated task than the traidtional rituals of primitive societies. Though this dissertation concentrates on the third point in Moore's scheme, it is clear that the length of time required to achieve the goals presented in points one and two has increased. I, like other social scientists, see the development of a stage between adolescence and adulthood as a necessary adaptation to a process that has become more difficult and time consuming than in earlier eras.

For most of man's history human life has been divided into two distinct stages: childhood and adulthood. The role of child or adult had, and still has, a fairly specific definition.

In primitive societies one of the basic functions of childhood was to prepare people for adulthood. A variety of factors, including slow rates of change and high visibility of role models, made the mastery of adult roles fairly easy to accomplish. As societies became more complex, preparation for adulthood became more difficult. An examination of certain aspects in the historical development of the adolescent stage can be instructive.

After the Civil War the United States experienced increased industrialization and urbanization. These changes made new skills more important and made the social order less stable (mobility in either direction was more possible). Under these conditions growing numbers of parents felt that the training they were giving their children was insufficient. More children than ever before were enrolled in secondary schools.

In 1872 a Supreme Court decision upheld the expenditure of public funds for secondary schools. During the 1870's bureaucracies developed to define and enforce educational standards, and teaching became a full-time career. By 1900 over half of the states in the union had cumpolsory school attendance laws: thus, the secondary school became institutionalized in order to better prepare its charges for adulthood.

The growth of high schools and urbanization led to the creation of a category of individuals who were at or past puberty but not working and had little freedom or independence. These people were not children but clearly were not adults. It was not until 1904 that G. Stanley Hall conceptualized "adolescence" and the teenage period was recognized as a new stage of life. (Keniston, 1971:4) Prior to that time puberty marked the end of childhood and the beginning of adulthood. Certainly, even after this conceptualization, many teenagers did not act as "adolescents." It should be kept in mind that it took more than a quarter of a century before adolescence was fully recognized as an accepted and expected stage of life. Some young people still worked, married, and supported families. However, education beyond elementary school was becoming increasingly important due to the growth of industrialization.(Keniston, 1971: 4) Teenagers were expected, then required, to stay in school Dating, eccentricities of dress, rebelliousness, stress, and other factors became associated with most people of this age category. Adolescence evolved and was recognized as a "new" stage in life which immediately preceded adulthood. It was in this stage that the young person was to be socialized to assume his or her adult role. At this point in time, adolescence was an example of how the growing complexity of society and increased demand for education created the need for an expanded period of prepatory socialization.

As a separate stage transadulthood has not yet been given societal acknowledgement. Nevertheless, a number of eminent scholars (Keniston, 1965; Parsons and Platt, 1972; Erickson, 1963; Flacks, 1971; and others) have already noted certain aspects of transadulthood. Their use of an ambiguous descriptive term, however, may engender some confusion. Keniston, and practically all the others, describe this stage as "youth." The confusion rests with the fact that youth is already understood to pertain to adolescence or late adolescence. Thus, the term "youth" seems to overlook the distinct nature of the new stage. Inherent in the term "transadulthood" is the implication of a new stage of life apart from adolescence. It refers to a transitional period between adolescence and adulthood.

A primary characteristic of the transadult is that responsibilities which are seen to be permanent are avoided or delayed. This does not mean that transadults are irresponsible. Many have been involved in assuming responsibilities and have worked hard to achieve. However, it is the lack of permanent commitment which differentiates the transadult from the adult. Perhaps the Peace Corps is one of the best examples of responsible, dedicated but not long-lasting involvement. In their article, "Higher Education and Changing Socialization," Parsons and Platt note that young people realize that a difinitive commitment to one area of involvement jeopardizes their opportunity or at least their potential for pursuing other areas. (Parsons and Platt, 1972:248)

Transadulthood must be clearly differentiated from adolescence. Most transadults do not live with their parents. They are not subject to the disciplines and constraints of high school. While the teenager is in the initial process of learning how to relate intellectually, emotionally and sexually with the opposite sex, transadults are beyond this initial stage. Transadults are more socially and psychologically sophisticated than teenagers. Their identities are more strongly established. They have more freedom to act independently. Unlike the deliberately rebellious adolescent, transadults are more likely to broaden their manner of relating to their parents and other elders. Adults are more apt to be viewed as multidimensional people, and their value system is more likely to be respected if not supported by the transadult. During this stage one becomes capable of questioning family traditions and parental lifestyles without necessarily negating them. The freedom to experiment with alternative living patterns may, at this point, be exercised.

Respondents in this sample indicated a very high level of respect for their parents. In only two cases did respondents indicate no respect for their parents, and only seven percent said they had little respect for parents. The vast majority, even when they indicated differing views on politics, drugs, or cohabitation, stated clearly that though they differed with their parents they were certainly capable of understanding their parents' perspective.

Just as transadults are not adolescents, they are not adults. They do not have the permanent commitments and responsibilities associated with adulthood. They are not married, are somewhat unsure of career plans, and in many cases consciously attempt to limit their material possessions. Essentially, they often hope to delay the acquisition of anything that would interfere with their flexibility.

For example, we find within the sample of the cohabiting couples an ambivalent attitude toward marriage and adulthood. They are not without desire for the supposed security of marriage, nor are they unaffected by parental reaction and society's pressure for them to conform; yet they are not prepared to make the commitments of adulthood. One must be careful, however, not to generalize about the attitudes of cohabitors. Certainly the very act of living together is a commitment, and for some a commitment seen as permanent. Yet most have seen their cohabitation as an experiment and/or a trial with permanent commitment still viewed as something which will occur in the future.

According to Keniston (1971:11), perspectives regarding death change with each stage of life. Individuals in the 18-30 age bracket perceive repetitive activities, lack of freedom, and being in a rut as symbolic of death. Since these activities are associated with adulthood, the transadult can be characterized as fostering an ambivalent attitude toward entering that stage. Though transadults often foresee themselves achieving affluence and high status (nearly seventy percent of the sample of respondents expected eventually to enter professional careers), they fear that the negative aspects of adulthood are incompatible with their present lifestyle. The world of the adult is viewed as meaningless, unattractive and, perhaps worse of all, boring.

It is important to note that deferment of adulthood is a choice that the individual makes rather than one which is demanded. Society does not bar transadults from adult status; rather, the individual declines entrance. Erikson's "psychological moratorium" concept suggests that this stage is a period during which commitments are delayed, thus allowing the person time to experiment with various roles and lifestyles. (Erikson, 1959) It is also a time in which the individual can work to achieve an inner unity and sense of self before commitment to adult roles. (Keniston, 1965:399)

In summary, the transadult, an individual in a transitional period between adolescence and adulthood, has the following characteristics: first, and most importantly, responsibilities which are conceived as permanent are avoided or delayed; a variety of experiences are sought, often with the hope that they will lead to the discovery of a suitable or desirable way of life; flexibility is of central importance; finally, transadulthood is marked by a certain amount of ambivalence toward adulthood. This period extends from entrance to college or the end of adolescence to that point at which the individual accepts himself or herself as an adult. It is a period of experimentation with different life styles, a searching for career orientation, and a time for testing educational goals. Transadulthood then involves a moratorium period in which marriage, permanent settlement, difinitive occupation, and other manifestations of adulthood are, in the interests of self-exploration, delayed.

The concept of differentiation can be usefully applied in order to understand the role of the transadult in a developmental sequence. Differentiation is the process in which a structure that performed a number of functions is subdivided into two or more structures which together performs the same functions. The development of new stages in the life cycle can best be conceptualized as a differentiation of the pre-adult period in the life cycle. According to Flacks (1971:11):

> The proportion of young in school and the length of time they are
> expected to remain there are greatly increased as industrial society
> evolves because this type of society requires that its members have an
> unprecedented degree of flexibility and mobility. The process of
> creating new types of work and phasing out old lines is continuous;
> the need for universal discipline, literacy, specialized training,
> and meritocratic competition steadily widens.

A number of scholars such as Margaret Mead, 1970; Philip Slater, 1970; and Alvin Toffler, 1970, plus others, believe that the post-industrial society is a marked departure from society just decades ago. These changes have again made adult roles more difficult to master and bring pressure for a further differentiation of the life cycle. Transadulthood may be understood as a response to these pressures. Whereas one stage of life is required to prepare a person for adulthood in pre industrial society (childhood), perhaps three are necessary in post-industrial society (childhood, adolescence, and transadulthood). In the late 1960's and early 1970's it appeared that young people were demanding more time to make commitments which are required of adults in our society. If we employ the example of the cohabiting couple one can clearly sense a delaying of adulthood, marriage and commitment rather than a re-placing of these institutions.

In her book Culture and Commitment: A Study of the Generation Gap, Margaret Mead describes the "youth culture" of the 1960's. She suggests that this culture is comprised, to a large extent, of the people from upper middle class backgrounds. Such individuals are usually the pace setters for the rest of the society. Those in the role of intellectual leadership, she claims, usually initiate innovations and make the first psychological adaptations to them. The task of integrating novelty with older values and institutions is presented to those elites. They provide in themselves models for others adapting to social change. (Mead, 1970)

The transadult can be viewed as an adaptation to a changing, increasingly complex society which demands a prolonged period of vocational training and educational expertise. The unmarried cohabitation of college students and graduate students can be viewed as one of the various ways in which these young people have integrated the new values with older institutions. We can view transadulthood as a functional necessity in a society which generates increasing demands for education. It appears, as well, that unmarried heterosexual cohabitation is a functionally efficient means of adapting the emotional and sexual needs of young people to a system that prolongs the period of nonadulthood in our society.

CHAPTER IV

THE COHABITORS

Background Information and
Social Characteristics

This section outlines the social characteristics of those involved in co-habiting relationships.

Marital Status

In Table 1 we see that 90 percent of those in the sample have never been married.* Only six of the males and five of the females have had previous legal marriages. In three cases divorced men were living with divorced or separated women. In two cases, children were involved. In both of these situations the woman's children (two in one case, one in the other) were living with the couple. In the one case where the young man is not legally separated from his first wife, he is living with a young woman who has never been married. The oldest couple in the study is part of this group. He is a divorced college teacher of 34, and she is a former kindergarten teacher of 33, recently separated and has just returned to graduate school.

TABLE 1. MARITAL STATUS OF INDIVIDUALS LIVING TOGETHER
(be Sex)

	%		
Marital Status	Male	Female	Total
Single	88	90	89
Married	2	0	1
Separated	4	4	4
Divorced	6	6	6
	100	100	100
	N=50	N=50	

Age

Age breakdown reveals that the males in the study are slightly older than the females. In both groups, however, the largest proportion fall in the age categories between 20 and 23, i.e., the last few years of college or first few years after graduation. Approximately two-thirds of the entire sample falls into this age grouping. Only one female was over 27, but five of the males, or one-tenth of those males in the sample, are over 27. In fact, only one female in the sample who was over 25 had ever been married.

_____

*I realize that the description of the findings in terms of percentages in an exploratory study of 50 couples may seem to exaggerate the importance of a small sample. However, it was my intention in this chapter to present as clear and exact a picture of the respondents as was possible.

TABLE 2. AGE OF RESPONDENTS IN UNMARRIED COUPLE SAMPLE
(by Sex)

Age	%		
	Male	Female	Total
18-19	10	16	13
20-21	40	48	44
22-23	22	24	23
24-25	14	6	10
26-27	4	4	4
28-29	6	0	3
30 or over	4	2	3
	100	100	100

Social Class

In terms of parent's occupation, a large percentage of the cohabitors come from middle and upper middle class backgrounds. Approximately 60 percent of the males and females classified their parents' income as over $16,000 a year. Approximately 30 percent said their parents made more than $25,000 a year and nearly 20 percent said their parents' income was over $30,000. Clearly these young people have come from homes where they could be well provided for, at least materially. Interestingly, less than 20 percent of the males and females stated that their mothers were housewives. Although many had only recently returned to part-time or full-time employment after their children were "off at school."

Respondents were asked to classify the social class in which they were raised. That question revealed the following information:

TABLE 3. SOCIAL CLASS IN WHICH RESPONDENT WAS RAISED
(by Sex)

Social Class	%		
	Male	Female	Total
Working	24	8	16
Middle	48	66	57
Upper Middle	28	26	27
	100	100	100
	N=50	N=50	N=100

The data indicates that the respondents themselves overwhelmingly considered themselves to have been brought up in the middle and upper middle classes (84 percent of the sample). Here we see some differentiation between the males and females. The women in the sample were three times less likely than the men to come from working class backgrounds.

Although we have obtained information on the respondent's income and perceived social class, the information is somewhat difficult to effectively tabulate and analyze since many of these young people are still students, under-graduates or graduates, and cannot realistically define their own present status situation.

38

Education

In terms of education we find these young people are definitely headed for or are already among the education elite. Thirty percent of the sample are college graduates, hold graduate degrees or are now in graduate school. Another 58 percent are now in college. Only 12 percent of the males and females in the sample did not continue their education beyond high school. Consequently a population which consists of individuals, 88 percent of whom have at least some college, must be considered a highly educated sample. As a further indication of their intellectual capabilities, 60 percent of the males and approximately 75 percent of the females stated that they graduated in the top 25 percent of their high school class.

Religion

Questions in this area revealed a number of interesting findings about the religious value structure and orientation of the respondents. Two tables are presented concerning religious preference of respondents and their parents' religious preference to put the analysis of this characteristic in the proper perspective.

TABLE 4. RELIGION OF RESPONDENTS AND THEIR PARENTS
(by Sex)

A. <u>Respondents</u>

	%		
Religion	Male	Female	Total
Catholic	8	6	7
Protestant	10	8	9
Jewish	12	20	16
Agnostic	20	14	17
Atheist	6	2	4
None	28	38	33
Other	16	12	14
	100	100	100
	N=50	N=50	N=100

B. Respondents' Parents

	%		
Religion	Male	Female	Total
Catholic	30.	20	24
Protestant	22	34	28
Jewish	36	38	37
Agnostic	0	2	1
Atheist	4	0	2
None	8	6	7
	100	100	100
	N=50	N=50	N=100

According to the responses, over 50 percent of the respondents classified themselves as either agnostics, atheists, or of no religion at all. In contrast, only 10 percent of their parents were similarly classified. In the interviews and the group discussions respondents talked at great length of their lack of religious involvement. In fact 80 percent of the respondents said that religion was not important to them. Although many agreed that organized religion is more of a burden than an enrichment or fulfilling experience, many felt that religious training was important for children. They talked of the identity religion supplies and of the teaching and learning that takes place in religious schools. One point that is quite clear is that many of these young people may return to the "practice" of their religion if and when they have children.

There was a good deal of discussion which centered around building one's own religious base, and often couples mentioned that some compromise such as the Unitarian Church might provide the kind of religious training with which they would be comfortable. Some were emphatic in stating that even if they did marry and have children they would not be involved with any religious structure. Obviously only time can answer that type of futuristic question; but my general feeling from the interviews was that many would return, at least to some extent, to organized religion.

The table below describes more exactly the combination of religious backgrounds and the frequencies in this sample.

TABLE 5. RELIGIOUS BACKGROUNDS

Religious Background		Absolute Frequency	Percentage
Male	Female		
Same religious background		15	30
Protestant	Catholic	3	6
Protestant	Jewish	5	10
Catholic	Protestant	7	14
Catholic	Jewish	4	8
Jewish	Protestant	5	10
Jewish	Catholic	2	4
Other mixed religious backgrounds		9	18
		N=50	100

This table was constructed by comparing the religious affiliation of the parents of the respondents rather than the respondents themselves. In this case I wanted to examine the similarity of their social backgrounds. The data also needs to be examined more carefully due to the manner in which religious background was categorized. Categories such as "agnostic," "atheist," and "none" are indicated on data cards in separate categories. Therefore, among the nine couples listed as "other religious backgrounds" there are five couples in which parental religious differences arise from a situation where, for example, the male categorized his parents as "atheists" while his partner categorized her parents as having no religious affiliation. If we reclassify those couples with similar religious backgrounds, the data reveals the following:

TABLE 6. SIMILARITY OF RESPONDENTS' PARENTS RELIGIOUS BACKGROUNDS

Religious Background	Absolute Frequency	Percentage
Similar religious background	20	40
Mixed religious background	30	60
	N=50	100

Politics

Among the many questions I was attempting to answer was that of how "radical" those involved in the unmarried couple alternative might be. In order to gather information about their political affiliations I asked each respondent to categorize himself in two ways. First, I asked whether they considered themselves Democrats, Republicans or Independents, and then asked them to classify themselves as either conservatives, moderates, liberals or radicals. Again, in order to better understand their backgrounds, respondents were asked to similarly classify their parents. The tables concerning that information are presented below, both for the respondents and for their parents.

TABLE 7. RESPONDENTS AND RESPONDENTS' PARENTS POLITICAL
PARTY PREFERENCE AND POLITICAL IDEOLOGY

A. Political Party Preference

Political Preference	Respondents	Parents
Democrat	24%	55%
Republican	2	19
Independent	64	23
Apathy	10	0
No answer	0	3
	100%	100%
	N=100	N=100

B. Political Ideology

Political Ideology	Respondents	Parents
Conservative	0%	17%
Moderate	13	51
Liberal	51	29
Radical	26	0
No answer	10	3
	100%	100%
	N=100	N=100

Table A presents political party preference for the respondents and their parents respectively. Table B presents the political ediology of the respondents and their parents. In Table A we notice the additional category of apathy. Those young people in this category stated that they were uninvolved in politics, that it was a "drag," that politics was something with which they did not wish to be bothered. These young people were not, however, typical of the group. A far larger proportion were, in fact, actively involved in working for candidates, voter registration, women's centers, tenants' union, against the war in Vietnam, and for a wide variety of reforms on college campuses. The majority of the sample (nearly two-thirds), all of whom were voting age as of January 1, 1973, classified themselves as independents. Of the entire sample of 100, not one female and only two males categorized themselves as Republicans. Approximately one-quarter of the young people did classify themselves as Democrats.

As we examine the party preference of their parents, there is clearly a greater majority of Democratic political backgrounds. In this sample 60 percent of the males and 50 percent of the females classified their parents' party preference as Democratic. In contrast to the 55 percent of the parents sample classified as Democratic, less than 20 percent of the respondents classified their parents as Republican. Before we predict that children of Democrats are more likely to experiment with alternatives than those of Republicans, let us examine the political ideology of our respondents and their parents. A review of the data concerning parents' political ideology reveals the following information:

TABLE 7A. PARENTS' POLITICAL PARTY PREFERENCE BY POLITICAL IDEOLOGY

Democrats
Conservative	4%
Moderate	31
Liberal	20

Republicans
Conservative	7
Moderate	12

Independents
Conservative	6
Moderate	8
Liberal	9

No Answer	3
	100%

For the entire parents' sample approximately half (51 percent) were categorized as moderates. Approximately 70 percent of the liberals in the sample were Democrats with the remainder categorized as Independents. In contrast to their parents, where less than 30 percent were classified as liberals and none as radicals, over 50 percent of the respondents considered themselves liberals with an additional 26 percent stating that they were radicals.

The interviews revealed that these young people were quite knowledgeable about politics and were "involved." Although none of the respondents classified themselves as conservatives, and only 13 percent as moderates, we should be aware that the liberal views of these young people are at least in part a function of age and education.

An interesting finding is that in almost 70 percent of the cases the parents of the couple have similar political party preference (i.e., if you are a Democrat and your daughter is involved in a living-together situation, you can be almost certain that his parents are Democrat, and so I'm sure we have eased the minds of many parents with this finding).

Community

The types and size of the communities in which these young people grew up offers further insight as to their backgrounds. The data points to the conclusion that a large majority were brought up in suburban communities close to large cities. This sample particularly reflects those brought up in the New York metropolitan area. Only five percent of the sample, three females and two males, said they lived more than 50 miles from a large city. Approximately 60 percent said they came from medium sized towns (10,000-25,000) or small cities (25,000-75,000). Everyone in the sample except one was born in the United States. That young man, born in South Africa, has been living in the United States for nine years.

Family Size

Another aspect of social background that I investigated was the size of the family of orientation (the family in which the child is raised). Ten percent of the sample, four males and six females, were the only children in their family (in no case was an only child paired with another only child). On the other end of the spectrum, six percent (three males and three females) came from families with eight or more children. However, the majority (70 percent) came from families that had two or three children.

I have presented information up to this point on the marital status, age financial status, social class, education, religion, political attitudes, type of community and family size of the respondents. This information is basic to understanding who they are and what background they bring into this social phenomenon of unmarried heterosexual cohabitation.

Relationship With Family

In this section I will examine the relationship between the respondents and their families.

Finances

The reported figures indicate that in at least half of the cases these young people are somewhat financially dependent on their parents. In fact, I believe these figures probably underestimate somewhat the amount of dependence on parents. As an example, a young man may state that he is financially independent, yet the interview will reveal that his father bought the car he is driving and pays the insurance. He accepts birthday and Christmas gifts in cash and put his last summer's plane fare to Europe on Dad's American Express Card. Aside from the underestimation of dependence, a number of interesting facts are brought to light. The women in the study are more dependent financially on their parents than are the males. This is in part due to the fact that they are younger, but it is also quite clear that independence, at least financially, is more important to the males in the study than the females. They seem to be somewhat more prone to exaggerate their independence and often wear it as a badge of success. Table 8 below indicates the financial relationship between the respondents and their parents.

TABLE 8. FINANCIAL RELATIONSHIP WITH PARENTS
(by Sex)

	%		
With Parents	Male	Female	Total
Independent	58	42	42
Partially dependent	34	46	40
Dependent	8	12	10
	100	100	100
	N=50	N=50	N=100

Parents' Relationship

I was interested in evaluating the respondents' view of their parents' marriage and establishing what percentage had come from "broken" homes. The data on marital continuity of parents reveals the following information:

TABLE 9. PARENTS' MARITAL STATUS WHILE RESPONDENT WAS GROWING UP
(by Sex)

| | % | | |
Marital Status of Parents	Male	Female	Total
Divorced	12	6	9
Separated	6	4	5
Widowed	10	4	7
No marital discontinuity	72	86	79
	100	100	100
	N=50	N=50	N=100

In Table 9 above we see that twice as many of the males compared to the females come from a "broken" home. However, less than 10 percent of the sample came from homes in which a divorce had taken place.

As a further test of the respondents' evaluation of their parents' marriage they were asked to classify their parents' marriage on a continuum from very happy to very unhappy. The results of that inquiry are presented in Table 10.

TABLE 10. RESPONDENTS' EVALUATION
OF PARENTS' MARRIAGE (by Sex)

| Marriage as Seen | % | | |
by Respondent	Male	Female	Total
Very happy	10	30	21
Happy	42	34	38
Neutral	24	28	26
Unhappy	14	4	9
Very unhappy	10	4	7
	100	100	100
	N=50	N=50	N=100

It seems that often there is an expectation that young people will negatively evaluate their parents' marriage. In fact, young people seem to expect other young people to see their own parents' marriage as dull, a life of conformity and "staying together because of the kids." A typical comment I heard quite frequently was, "I guess I'm a bit unusual; I really think my parents have a good and happy marriage."

Respect

I expected that parents might be in disagreement with the concept of unmarried heterosexual cohabitation. Since I expected a difference in values I wanted to know how much respect the young people in the study had for their parents. I realize that the use of such words as happiness or respect are extremely difficult to interpret. The meaning of these words is certainly different to different poeple, yet I feel

44

that answers to questions like these supply us with a good general picture of the group. Table 11 presents the responses I received to the question, "How much respect do you have for your parents?"

TABLE 11. AMOUNT OF RESPECT FOR PARENTS (by Sex)

Level of Respect	Male	Female	Total
		%	
A great deal	48	54	51
Some	40	40	40
Little	10	4	7
None	2	2	2
	100	100	100
	N=50	N=50	N=100

Over half of the respondents indicated that they had a great deal of respect for their parents. It is often the case that parents and young people are not adept at communicating their feelings to each other. In a number of cases young people who stated that they had a great deal of respect for their parents either implied or stated that their parents would probably not think that it was true. Moreover, parents who do respect the views and values of their children often fail to make their children aware of that respect.

Although this is admittedly only a speculation on my part, and I did not generally interview parents of respondents, my conversations with them led me to believe that they certainly felt their children to be quite capable of making responsible adult judgements. It is interesting to note that the two individuals who stated they had no respect for their parents were living together. Both are over 30; he is divorced and she is separated from her husband.

Although I have no systematic data on this area, it appears that the younger people in the sample were very converned about being honest and open with their parents. As an example, parents were often told of living arrangements not because of a desire to rebel, but rather because the young people involved wanted their parents to understand what they were doing and why.

Parental Knowledge and Reaction

An area of particular interest in this section is the manner in which respondents and parents interact concerning the cohabitation situation. I attempted to explore this area in a number of ways. An initial step in revealing the type of interaction between parents and respondents was to ask those involved in cohabiting relationships if their parents were aware that their children were involved in a nonmarital living-together arrangement. In Table 12 I present the data indicating the level of awareness, according to respondents, that their parents have concerning their living arrangements.

45

TABLE 12. PARENTS' KNOWLEDGE OF COHABITATION
ACCORDING TO RESPONDENT (by Sex)

Parents' Knowledge	%		
	Male	Female	Total
Yes	74	54	64
Know but do not acknowledge the fact	12	22	17
No	14	24	19
	100	100	100
	N=50	N=50	N=100

Some explanation of the categories involved in Table 12 is necessary. Under the category Yes I include parents who were specifically told by their son or daughter as well as parents who were made aware of the situation in any other way. As one male member of a couple put it, "My parents call often and after Carole answered the phone a few times, particularly at odd hours or when I wasn't home, it didn't take great intuition to figure out what was going on." John, like many of the males in the study, did not try to hide that fact that he was living with Carole, but he did not openly tell his parents until they specifically asked. Paula took a different means of informing her parents. Before she moved in with Art she went home for two weeks on a vacation, explained to them what she planned to do, and gave them time to react to the situation before the fact. Another respondent put it this way: "My father and mother both know. He even comes to visit us. He likes Tom and Tom likes him but try to talk to my mother about and she either cries or goes to her room." Seventy-four percent of the males and 54 percent of the females stated that heir parents were aware of their living arrangements.

The second category includes those young people who stated that they were sure their parents knew exactly what was going on but it was not discussed. Respondents who were assigned to this category indicated that their parents never specifically asked and no explanation or information was offered. As one young woman put it,

I know they know, and they know I realize they are aware of
my living situation, but it would hurt them to openly confronted
with it. I don't say anything about it and neither do they. When
Gary and I visit them for a weekend or something we don't
sleep together. I think it's really ridiculous, but that the
way it is.

Similar statements were made by males concerning their means of dealing with their parents.

At the beginning of the year when Nancy moved into my place she
was afraid to tell her parents and kept her dorm room all this
year. I wasn't sure what to tell my parents so I just didn't
say anything. Neither of us goes home for more than a day or two
on vacations, then we come back here to be together. I'm sure
that my folks know what's happening but we just don't talk about
it. I told my younger brother who is 16 and although he says he
hasn't said anything I know he has. My folks don't bother me
about it so I just leave well enough alone.

One respondent said, "My mother definitely knows but I'm not sure if my father knows or not." Twelve percent of the males and 22 percent of the females characterized their parents' awareness of their living arrangement in this way.

The final category, 14 percent of the males and 24 percent of the females, stated that their parents did not know they were involved in a cohabitation relationship. In a few cases they stated that their parents lived out of state and they just never bothered to tell them.

My parents live in West Virginia and my father is retired. I don't tell them because I know they would disapprove and be unnecessarily upset. I keep my own little apartment even though I live with Nick so I get my mail there. This relationship probably won't last long so why put them through that hassle.

The women in this group often state that the reason they don't tell their parents is that "knowing" would "hurt" them. As Barbara put it, "A long time ago I found out that some things are better left unsaid." In some cases, however, girls know from previous experience that it is better not to be open about the situation to their parents.

They stopped speaking to me when they found out about the last guy I was living with. We had told them (that we were living together). We (my parents and I) got back on speaking terms after that relationship ended. Now it's not worth the emotional upheaval of telling them about this new situation but probably (we) will if it gets very heavy.

The figures reveal that the male's parents are more likely to be aware of the situation than the female's. However, 76 percent of the females said that their parents were aware of the situation although 22 percent of these parents did not "officially" acknowledge the relationship. In cases where parents did not know, some made a conscious effort to hide the situation while others merely left the fact unsaid. As mentioned above, a few of the girls maintained dorm rooms for the entire year which they never used except when parents came to visit. In some cases two apartments were kept although the couple always stayed together in one of them. In one interesting case a number of single people and two couples were living communally. When one of the male's parents came to visit, all the female undergarments, etc., would be hidden and vice versa when a female's parents came to visit. Whether this intrigue was successful or not was uncertain, but they said they all had a good time at it, though they suspected that their parents knew what was going on. Finally, in one case, a couple actually had two phones in the apartment; one for him and one for her. He never answered hers, and she did not answer his. In fact, last summer when her mother came to visit, they took all of his things out of the apartment and he went to live with a friend during the time of her mother's visit. Apparently, in over 80 percent of the cases the parents do, in fact, have knowledge of the situation. Their reaction to the situation will be discussed shortly.

As a step beyond whether their parents are aware of the situation I was interested to discover if they, as a couple, interact with their parents. I therefore posed two questions about their visiting habits. I wondered if the couple visited the parents and whether the parents visited the couple. The two tables below present that information.

TABLE 13. DOES THE COUPLE VISIT PARENTS?

	Yes	No
Male	(40) 80%	(10) 20%
Fem.	(41) 82%	(9) 18%
Total	81%	19%

TABLE 14. DO PARENTS VISIT THE COUPLE?

	Yes	No
Male	(23) 46%	(27) 54%
Fem.	(27) 44%	(28) 56%
Total	45%	55%

These tables suggest that the living arrangements of cohabitors does not necessitate a severing of their relationship with their parents. The fact that over 80 percent of the respondents said that they, as a couple, visit their parents is really quite remarkable. However, this does not imply that they are treated as "a couple" in their parents' homes. In only a minority of the cases does the couple sleep together in the parents' house. In many cases, when visiting parents separate, sleeping quarters are provided. As one young man put it, "They know I"ll be headed into the bedroom as soon as they close the door but my mother still opens the convertible sofa in the living room and makes up the bed." In some cases, however, parents are extremely accommodating.

We had been living together at college for a few months before the summer break. I live in Washington, D.C. and Jerry's folks are on the West Coast. Jerry didn't really want to go home so my father got him a job in Washington. We lived together (had our own bedroom) at my parents house and stayed with them for the whole summer.

Parents, although they do visit the couple, are far less likely to do so than to have the couple visit them. Obviously a number of factors are involved. Vacations are often spent at home with the family and one member of the couple will bring a partner along. If parents come to visit the couple there is nowhere for them to stay. But probably the most important the food, the laundry service, and the costs to pay for these and other items are far more available at the parents' home. As one female respondent reported,

Actually I see my parents much more now than before Larry and I were living together. We go down there for weekends quite often. My father usually pays if we go out to dinner, and when we come back we usually have a substantial 'care package' from Mom.

I have briefly outlined the parents' knowledge of the unmarried couple and their visiting habits, but I have not yet described parental reaction to cohabitation. What do the parents think of their "little girl living in sin"? Are fathers knocking down doors with shotguns? What happens when Mom finds out Jane is living with a young man to whom she is not married? What of Joe's parents; do they approve or disapprove?

The data indicates that the majority of parents do not approve of premarital cohabitation, but they find themselves in a particularly difficult situation. Though they don't want to give approval to the relationship, they do not wish to cut themselves off from their children. Therefore, the situation frequently exists in which parents don't approve, but the disapproval takes the form of pressuring for marriage or separation without threatening their child or the relationship. Parents increasingly realize that standards have changed and that they have relatively little control over the actions of youngsters at the college age and beyond. It appears that although parents generally do not approve of this behavior, when faced with the choice of either accepting the situation or cutting themselves off from their child they choose to do the former. The following comments from respondents were typical:

"My parents are disappointed, I guess, but they don't entirely disagree."

"They know we are living together and even came to visit us, but they don't like the idea that we aren't married."

"They are against the basic idea, yet they tolerate it and treat us as married."

"They are not happy about it, but they believe we'll get married soon."

I have categorized the answers respondents gave to questions concerning reaction to their cohabitation in Table 15 below:

TABLE 15. EFFECT ON RELATIONSHIP BETWEEN PARENTS AND SONS OR DAUGHTERS (DUE TO PARENTS' REACTION TO COHABITATION - by Sex)

Result of Parental Reaction on Relationship with Parents	%		
	Males	Females	Total
Causes difficulties	18	36	27

48

TABLE 15. continued

Result of Parental Reaction on Relationship with Parents	%		
	Males	Females	Total
Better relationship	12	12	12
No difference	56	28	42
Parents don't know	14	24	19
	100	100	100
	N=50	N=50	N=100

Obviously the double standard is still quite apparent. Twice as many of the females (36 percent) stated that their parents' knowledge of this living situation caused problems in her relationship with them. But in only one case for the females did the parents actually stop communicating with their daughter. On the male side, in one case the father will no longer talk to his son, but the son does keep in touch with his mother on a regular basis. Furthermore, it was apparent that most of the young people in this study did not expect that their parents would cut them off either financially or emotionally because of their living situation.

In those cases when the reaction causes difficulties, how are these difficulties described? One female described her interaction with her mother saying,

When my mother found out I was living with Fred, she would not talk
to me at all. She doesn't like him and never has. We have been
together now for two years and she still doesn't speak to him.
I talk to her now on the phone and even visit once in awhile, but
she won't discuss the fact that Fred and I are living together.

In one interesting case the female's father was very understanding (even signing the lease so they could get an apartment together), but the male's father thought "that woman" had led his son away from his "good Catholic upbringing." The male's father called her names and even threatened her with physical violence. Today his father no longer considers him part of the family and has completely cut him off financially and emotionally. In this case both the male and the female involved were sophomores in college. Usually, according to respondents, parents who voice their disapproval say, in one form or another, "If you're going to live together, get married." Females more than males, as might be expected, receive more pressure to marry, but both are often pushed to either marry or be separated. In one case, however, when the daughter told her mother she planned to be married, her mother suggested they just continue living together. The mother did not approve of the young man and thought if they just lived together her daughter would soon see the light and leave him.

Interestingly 12 percent of the sample, six males and six females, stated that their relationship with their parents had improved with the parents' knowledge of the living-together relationship. In a number of cases the males stated that their parents saw this as a step toward greater maturity or responsibility.

My parents think Janet is terrific. I think they like her better than me.
My father always thought I was a bum, but now he knows I'm doing better
in school, eating better, using less drugs and living a far more stable existence.

Another factor that is often associated with living together is assuming more of the financial burden. For example, a female respondent stated,

When Barry and I started living together we decided we would no longer
accept financial support from our parents although they can probably
afford it. We got loans and both of us have part-time jobs. My folks
don't really like the fact that we are not married, but for the first
time in my life they really treat me like an adult and have a great
deal more respect for my opinions.

Although cohabitation was more apt to cause difficulties with parents than im-

49

prove the relationship, in most cases the reactions of parents were usually not as bad as expected. Laura recalled,

We worried for six months about how to tell my parents. For half a year I kept a dorm room even though we had an apartment together. When I finally told them their reaction was quite reasonable. I guess I didn't realize how much they respected my judgement. If I hadn't old them I think our relationship would have been strained to the breaking point.

TABLE 16. PARENTS' REACTION TO THEIR CHILDREN LIVING
IN AN UNMARRIED COHABITATION RELATIONSHIP
(ONLY FOR PARENTS AWARE OF THE RELATIONSHIP) (by Sex)

Result of Reaction on Relationship with Parents	%		
	Males	Females	Total
Causes difficulties	21	47	33
Better relationship	14	16	16
No difference	65	37	51
	100	100	100
	N=43	N=38	N=81

Of those parents who were aware of the situation, only about 20 percent of the males stated that parents' reaction caused difficulties in his relationship with them. On the other hand nearly half (47 percent) of the women stated that their parents' awareness caused problems. As can be seen from Table 16, a majority of the males (65 percent) said parents' knowledge did not affect his relationship with them. In some of these cases the males stated that the relationship was already bad before he became a part of a cohabiting couple. From the female viewpoint 37 percent of the young women stated that their relationship with parents had not been altered due to parents' awareness of her living-together arrangement.

However, though few respondents of either sex indicated that they felt "guilty" because of their living situation, females were more likely to express some feeling of guilt due to their cohabitation. As one female respondent stated, "I used to have what I thought was a very close relationship with my father, but ever since he found out about our living together he gets this sad, sad look on his face whenever I see him."

What of the other side of the coin? Does parental reaction in any way affect the relationship of those living together? This question is of particular interest to parents. If parental disapproval is present, what effect does this disapproval have on the cohabiting couple? In conversations I had with a number of married couples (not part of this sample) that had formerly been living together, they mentioned that at least part of the reason they married was to satisfy their parents by adding a legal contract to their relationship. In examining the information obtained from the respondents I found that only two of the males and four of the females stated that their relationship with their partner or mate suffered due to parental reaction. A female respondent complained,

I am constantly hassled by my folks to get married. Frank says he definitely doesn't want to get married yet and I just don't know. We don't exactly fight about it but it does cause problems. I really wouldn't care if it wasn't for my parents.

The male's parents may also directly or indirectly cause problems. I've already mentioned the case in which the young man's father threatened his partner, but it can be an indirect "hassle" for the couple. A male respondent explained,

When we started living together we agreed to split finances down
   the middle, but my father doesn't think I should get an allowance
   if I'm living with someone. I agree with him but since she still
   gets an allowance it's hard for me to keep my half and we do get
   into hassles about money.

   Parental reactions for the majority of the respondents do not, however, ad-
versely affect the relationship. Even when faced with emphatic disapproval, respondents did not feel that their relationship with the person they were living
with was damaged. In a few cases, in fact, the opposite was true. An example, perhaps,
is what Richard Driscoll and his colleagues call "the Romeo and Juliet effect."
(Driscoll, et al., 1970) If parents show disapproval, this can have a tendency to
bring the couple even closer.

   Since my parents don't approve of our relationship and don't
   want me to bring Steve to the house we go our own way on
   vacations. Having to sort of make it on our own seems to have
   made our relationship even better.

As another female respondent explained,

   My parents once came home from a vacation early and caught
   us together in their bed. Since then they haven't allowed
   him in the house and definitely wanted me to stop seeing
   him. That didn't work, of course. In fact, it probably had
   a lot to do with why we started living together in the first
   place and that was three years ago.

   Some parents, on the other hand, did react favorably. One female stated, "My
parents trust my judgement and think it's probably not a bad idea to try it before
getting married." A male respondent explained his parents would have a difficult
time voicing any disapproval.

   I guess my father would have to approve and he does. He and
   my mother were divorced while I was growing up. He has been
   living with a woman for five years. Almost everybody thinks
   they are married, but they are just living together.

Parents of cohabitors occasionally tell their children that they wish they were
young now when everything is more open and free. In fact, although it is difficult
to estimate the percentages, many of these young people believe that although parents
disapprove, they (they parents) have to admit that in many ways living together before
marriage does have some advantages.

Other relatives

   As another measure of how much the individual's family is aware of his or her
living arrangements, I asked respondents to tell me whether their aunts and uncles
or grandparents were aware of their living arrangements. The continuum is clearly in
a downward direction. As mentioned above, about 80 percent of the parents know.
Only about 40 percent of the aunts and uncles, and about 20 percent of the grandparents
were aware of the cohabitation relationship. Table 17 and 18 present data for aunts
and uncles, and grandparents respectively.

TABLE 17. AUNTS' AND UNCLES' AWARENESS OF COHABITATION (by Sex)*

Knowledge of Relationship	%		
	Male	Female	Total
Yes	48	36	42
No	52	64	58
	100	100	100
	N=50	N=50	N=100

TABLE 18. GRANDPARENTS' AWARENESS OF COHABITATION (by Sex)*

Knowledge of Relationship	%		
	Male	Female	Total
Yes	28	14	21
No	64	82	73
No answer, or all deceased	8	4	6
	100	100	100
	N=50	N=50	N=100

*If any aunts, uncles or grandparents knew, answer coded yes.

The data for awareness among parents, aunts and uncles, and grandparents consistently show the male's family was more likely to be aware of his living arrangements than was the female's family.

As a final question concerning the couple's relationship with their individual families I asked if they attended "family fatherings" where relatives were aware of the living situation. By relatives I meant more than just parents. Again, when the cohabiting couple did attend "family gatherings" they were more likely to be the male's family than the female's. The exact figures and percentages are presented in Table 19.

TABLE 19. ATTENDANCE AT FAMILY GATHERINGS WHERE RELATIVES
ARE AWARE OF THE COUPLE'S RELATIONSHIP (by Sex)

Attends Family Gatherings	%		
	Male	Female	Total
Yes	52	38	45
No	48	62	55
	100	100	100
	N=50	N=50	N=100

The Living Arrangement:
Where and How They Live

In this section I present findings that can be considered characteristic of the couple rather than of the two individuals. The data is divided into a number of sub-headings and provides answers to questions concerning their living situation, the type of community in which they live, their financial arrangement, as well as the manner in which household chores are allocated.

Living Situation

Table 20 presents the categorization of the living situations of the couples. A number of these categories will need some clarification. Those in apartments by themselves refers to just what the label implies: that the couple is renting an apartment and does not share it with any other roommates. The "apartment shared" category refers to those couples who have roommates. Typically, one member of the couple was already living in the apartment with a roommate of the same sex before the cohabiting couple relationship was established. The third category, "house by them-selves," is again what is implied: the couple lives in a single family house without other roommates. The "house shared" category indicates a communal arrangement in the two cases in this sample: the cohabiting couples were living in houses that were shared by other couples and individuals. In one case the house was shared by nine people, two couples both involved in a cohabitation relationship (only one couple is part of this sample), three single males and two single females. All were students at a college in the neighboring town. The second couple that was sharing a house lived with seven people consisting of three couples and one male (again only one of the three couples is part of this sample). The fifth category abbreviated as "house couple" describes a cohabiting couple who share a house with a married couple in a suburban neighborhood. They did not consider their arrangement communal although they often shared meals and socialized together. In the final category are those couples who were living together in dormitory rooms. Although cohabitation is not strictly legal, 24-hour visitation is allowed; therefore, enforcing restrictions against cohabitation is particularly difficult. The data is presented in the table below.

TABLE 20. LIVING SITUATION OF COHABITING COUPLES

Living Arrangement	Absolute Frequency	Percentage
Apartment by themselves	27	54
Apartment shared	14	28
House by themselves	1	2
House shared	2	4
House couple	1	2
Dormitory	5	10
	N=50	100%

As can be seen from Table 20, somewhat over half the couples did live in apart-ments by themselves. However, an additional 34 percent, just over one-third of the sample, shared their home with roommates or other couples. Finally, 10 percent of the sample were couples who were living together in dormitories. The dormitory couples represent an interesting finding in that the school and even the legislators may realistically have some control over that particular social phenomenon.

Type of Community

I categorized the type of community in which the couple lived and secured the following results. More than half of the sample, 54 percent of the couples, lived in urban working class and lower class neighborhoods. Frequently they rented part of a two or three-family house. Twenty percent of the sample lived in suburban areas, and four percent (two couples) lived in rural areas. The reader will notice that although I listed only five couples as living in dormitories in Table 20, seven couples, or 14 percent of those in the sample, list their neighborhood as dormitories. This is explained by the fact that many universities offer self-contained apartments in dormitories for use by graduate students who serve as residential counselors or advisors. Two of the cohabiting couples in the sample were serving in that capacity. They, therefore, had an apartment to themselves and yet lived within the dormitory. Table 21 below summarizes the findings on this topic.

TABLE 21. TYPE OF COMMUNITY IN WHICH COHABITING COUPLES LIVE

Community (Neighborhood)	Absolute Frequency	Percentage
Urban middle class	4	8
Urban working class	22	44
Urban lower class	5	10
Suburban middle class	7	14
Suburban working class	3	6
Rural	2	4
Dormitory	7	14
	N=50	100%

It is somewhat difficult to generalize about the answers received to the question: do your neighbors know you are living together without being married? Certainly in most cases some neighbors do and some don't; however, fully 80 percent of the couples stated that their neighbors knew they were not married. Many mentioned particular incidences when neighbors found out.

Someone knocked on Mrs. Jakowski's door downstairs and asked for me and gave my right name. At first Mrs. J. said, 'You have the wrong house,' but after she asked my friend to describe me she knew exactly who I was.

Many of the couples make no pretense at all of being married and carefully put both names on the door or mailbox. No couple in the sample mentioned any trouble with neighbors because they weren't married; but quite a few mentioned the difficulties they had in obtaining an apartment without being married. Most couples told the landlord they were married and then hoped he would not throw them out if he discovered they were not. A male respondent explained,

When we first moved in I told the landlord we were married, but after a week Susan started getting mail addressed to her own name. We considered saying we had just been married and lots of her friends still didn't know, but we decided instead to tell the truth and hope for the best. He said he wanted us out, but after we talked for awhile he said he'd think about it. That was the last we ever heard of it and we've been here seven months now.

In some cases, as mentioned before, fathers were willing to sign the lease and some even paid the rent. "My father was great about it. We never even get a bill. He (father) just mails a check each month for the rent."

Financial Arrangements

One of the facts of life for these couples, as well as for everyone else, is that the rent must be paid and food must be purchased. How do these couples share the financial burden? Do they keep their money in the same bank account?

Sixty percent of the cases (30 couples) stated that they shared equally in paying the bills. In addition 36 percent of the cases (18 couples) stated that bills were shared on an "ability to pay" basis. If the female was working while the male was a student, she was more apt to carry a larger portion of the financial burden; if the female was still a student while the male was in a full-time position, he then was more apt to pay a larger portion of the bills. In only one case did the male carry the entire financial load, and in one case the female did. In the case where the male paid for everything the female had to cover the cost for a room and food plan she wasn't using. In the case where the female paid all the bills the situation was described as "temporary" because her partner was unemployed.

Although 30 of the couples stated that they shared economic responsibilities equally, only 15 of the couples said they had equal incomes. In fact, males were almost twice as likely to make more money than females. Perhaps it is part of the new women's movement or perhaps the egalitarian ideal is followed at least economically; but even when salaries are unequal, cohabiting couples often divide their expenses equally.

As another aspect of the economics of living together I asked if the couples kept their money in the same bank account. Aside from the fact that many informed me that they has do little money it didn't matter, a very clear majority (72 percent) did not keep their money in the same bank account. Some explained that not having their money in the same account helped them in maintaining their individuality. They did not always have to ask the other if individual purchases were desired. Others stated that although they contributed equally to the things they did together, they didn't see any reason to keep their funds in the same account. A few of the couples explained that they kept joint accounts and individual accounts. As one female partner of a couple put it,

> Actually we have six different accounts. I have a savings and
> checking account of my own. He has a savings and checking account,
> and we (together) have a checking and savings account. We use
> our checking account for regular bills and our savings account
> for vacations we plan together.

The data concerning financial status or arrangements is presented in Table 22 A, B, and C.

TABLE 22. FINANCIAL ARRANGEMENTS OF COHABITING COUPLES

A. How are the expenses divided?

Who Pays (Food, Rent, etc.)	Absolute Frequency	Percentage
Equally divided	30	60
Share on ability	18	36
Male pays	1	2
Female pays	1	2
	N=50	100%

B. Which partner earns more?

Who earns more	Absolute Frequency	Percentage
Female	12	24
Male	23	46
Equal	15	30
	N=50	100%

C. Does the couple keep their money in the same bank account?

Same Account	Absolute Frequency	Percentage
Yes	14	28
No	36	72
	N=50	100%

Allocation of Household Chores

Another practicality of everyday life that interested me was the manner in which household responsibilities were divided. I wanted to evaluate whether cohabiting couples divided household chores along traditional "sexist" lines or if a more egalitarian concept was at work. Did the woman cook, clean and wash dishes and the man take out the garbage, or were tasks more equally divided? The data reveals that couples ranged from carefully planned egalitarianism to traditional sex role orientation. In one apartment I visited the kitchen wall contained a chart of all aspects of the week's responsibilities. Each meal was accounted for, as well as who would clean what and when it would be done. In that case both of the partners were students and both felt it was an important part of their relationship to have equal division of labor and responsibility. On the other end of the spectrum there was one case where the male was a full-time student and the female worked 40 hours a week on a full-time job. Although she worked full time, she still cooked the meals, washed the dishes, did the laundry and kept the apartment clean. The male in this case stated that he was responsible for "the heavy work." This actually included taking out the garbage and working on the car if something went wrong.

Although individual cases might be argued one way or the other, my classification reveals that in 70 percent of the cases household responsibilities were sex-role oriented. Furthermore, an age factor was an important variable in this classification. Generally the younger couples were more likely to have egalitarian relationships in terms of household responsibilities.

The Relationship

Formation and Duration

As one means of evaluating the relationship between the young men and women in the sample I wanted to find out how strong a relationship they had before they started living together. Table 23 describes the length of time respondents stated they were involved with each other preceding the time they began cohabiting. The range went from one night to almost five years. One couple stated they met at a dorm dance. They stayed in his dorm room that night and she never really left. As she put it,

We started living together immediately after that first night.
Since then I think I've only spent two nights in my own dorm
room. I guess you could call it love at first sight.

At the other end of the spectrum, one couple said they started dating at age 15 and were "going together" for a long time before they finally made the decision to live together on a full-time basis in their sophomore year at college. Interestingly, this couple also stated that he used to want to get married, but Laura is a staunch feminist and believes marriage is a degrading institution for the female. As she put it, "Mark and I both want to do a great deal of traveling and have careers. Children just aren't possible under those circumstances." A review of Table 23 reveals a number of interesting aspects about the sample of cohabitors.

TABLE 23. LENGTH OF RELATIONSHIP BEFORE STARTING TO LIVE TOGETHER

Period of Time	Absolute Frequency	Percentage
Less than 1 month	6	12
1 - 3 months	11	22

TABLE 23 continued

Period of Time	Absolute Frequency	Percentage
4 - 6 months	5	10
7 - 12 months	13	26
13 months - 2 years	7	14
3 - 5 years	8	16
	N=50	100%

Although occasionally this type of relationship occurs very soon after these young people meet, that occurrence is by no means typical of the sample. Only six couples had been involved with each other less than a month before they started living together. The majority (56 percent) had had a relationship for at least seven months before they started living together. And 30 percent of the sample had been "going together" for more than a year prior to establishing a living-together relationship. Obviously for most of these young people the decision to live together was not a quick one. Many, in fact, stated that they never consciously made a decision to live together, it just happened. For example, Steve stated,

I began spending most of my nights at Leslie's place and before we
realized it I was spending all of my nights there. I never moved my
things over, but occasionally I would need something and bring it
over. I just stopped taking things back to my place.

On the other hand some of the couples planned their living together for months in advance.

We met in April last year and often stayed together in the dorm room.
We knew before school was over that we wanted to be together next
year even though we both had to live at home for the summer. I arranged
to 'live' with three other girls. Of course they knew in advance
that I would never be there and Paul got a two bedroom place with a
friend of his and we shared the rent three ways. It was all arranged
before we even left for summer vacation.

We can now examine the period of time that the couples in this sample have been cohabiting. The median time that these couples have been living together is between 10 and 12 months. Forty-four percent (22) of the couples have been together for more than a year; this figure includes five couples who have been together more than two years. Considering the young age of the respondents in the sample, these couples have been together for a substantial period of time. Only one couple in the sample had been together for less than two months. The female in this couple has recently moved into her partner's apartment but they both stated that they "definitely" plan to stay together "for a long time." The longest any of the couples in the sample had been together is three years, and six percent of the sample, or three couples, fall into that category. Nearly 70 percent of the couples had been living together at least seven months at the time of the interview. Table 24 below presents the length of time the couples have been cohabiting.

TABLE 24. DURATION OF COHABITING RELATIONSHIP AT THE TIME OF INTERVIEW

Period of Time Cohabiting	Absolute Frequency	Percentage
Less than 1 month	1	2
1 - 2 months	2	4
3 - 4 months	5	10
5 - 6 months	8	16
7 - 9 months	5	10

TABLE 24. continued

Period of Time Cohabiting	Absolute Frequency	Percentage
10 - 12 months	7	14
13 months - 2 years	17	34
More than 2 years	5	10
	N=50	100%

Breakups and Vacations

Another aspect of the cohabiting relationship which I explored with these couples was the amount of disruption the couple might have had in their relationship. I wanted to know if for any reason the couple either decided to or had to break up" for a period of time since they initiated a cohabitation relationship. In 12 cases, or 24 percent of the couples, some break in the relationship had taken place, but most of these were not due to "difficulties" in the relationship. In five instances one or both partners moved home with his or her family for the summer. In two cases, however, one partner moved home while the other spent the summer traveling in Europe. In both cases the other partner needed to stay home to work and the break was agreed to by both parties. In four cases the break was triggered by difficulties or problems. Arguments led to the temporary dissolution of the relationship in two cases. In the first situation the male member felt that he should be the decision maker for the couple, his partner disagreed and he decided at that point to walk out. After a few months they mutually decided to re-establish a cohabiting relationship but the "disagreement" has not clearly been settled. They have been living together for three years, and the break came shortly after their first year together. The second situation in which arguments caused a disruption in cohabitation was one in which the couple had been living together in his dormitory room. When they argued she would leave and return to her own dorm room. They explained that this has happened three or four times, but it never lasts for more than a few days. They have been living together for seven months. Insecurity was labeled as the cause of breakups in two of the relationships. In both cases the female's parents were very unhappy about their daughter's situation. In one case the daughter went to live at home for four months. In the other, the young woman took a trip to the West Coast. In both cases the couple was reunited.

Vacations are another aspect of interruptions in relationship. I wondered if these young couples always vacationed together or did they go separately. Excluding those who go "home" to parents for summer vacation, the data reveals that about a third of the couples do sometimes take separate vacations. In most cases, however, it seems they do not take separate vacations because they want to, but rather because of scheduling difficulties or job responsibilities. Charles reported, "I'm in grad school and she has a full-time job, so when I have a vacation from school sometimes I'll go to visit friends or go lay in the sun." In a samll minority of the cases separate vacations was what the couple desired. For example, one female stated,

We sometimes think it's good to get away for awhile. You appreciate
each other more when you get back. We go different places to get a
change to miss each other.

In other situations parental attitudes demanded separate vacations. "Paula goes home sometimes and I can't go with her because her parents just aren't ready to handle the situation." But these young couples, for the most part, neither desire nor take separate vacations. Excluding again those going home for the summer, 60 percent of the couples said they never take separate vacations.

A Typology of Unmarried
Heterosexual Relationships

In the initial stages of the formulation of this project I had a great many informal discussions with young people who either were cohabiting or had had experience in a cohabitation relationship. In these discussions, as well as in interviews conducted in connection with a former study (Danziger, 1971), it became apparent that cohabitors could not be considered a homogeneous group; that couples differed in their definition of the situation, their level of commitment and their plans for the future. As a part of this research I tried to clarify the various levels of the bond that existed between the partners involved in cohabitation relationships. Having discussed this matter with a great many couples I developed a five-part typology which characterized the various levels of commitment in unmarried heterosexual cohabitation arrangements. Before I present the findings for this particular sample I will define the clarification scheme.

I have labeled the categories of cohabiting relationships as casual, transitory, stable, trial marriage, and alternative to marriage. The casual couple is characterized by the fact that although they are living together, they do not consider their relationship to be exclusive and have vague plans for the future. "Casual" couples state that they do "date" other people and had agreed to this type of relationship before they started living together. The couples that have been categorized as "transitory" are those who consider their relationship exclusive, at least for the time being, but have very vague ideas or plans about the future. The third category is that which I have labeled a "stable" relationship. These couples consider their relationship to be quite stable, believe that they will be living together for some time into the future and, in most cases, say that their relationship is exclusive (i.e., they do not date others). The "trial marriage" is characterized by those who state in one way or another what Terry and Elaine said:

We are thinking of marriage in the future and we want to find
out if we really are what each other wants. If everything works
out we will be getting married.

The final category is reserved for those who consider their relationship to be a "permanent" alternative to marriage. These couples say they will probably spend the rest of their lives together but do not plan to marry.

In the questionnaire respondents were asked: "Which of the following statements best describes your relationship?"

___We are living together, but ours is not an exclusive relationship; both of us date other people and our plans for the future are vague. (Casual)

___We are living together and for the time being our relationship is exclusive. However, our plans for the future are vague. (Transitory)

___We consider our relationship to be very stable and we can foresee living together for some time into the future. (Stable)

___We consider our relationship a trial marriage. (Trial Marriage)

___We consider our relationship an alternative to marriage. (Alternative)

The modal category contains 40 percent of the couples; these cohabitors considered theirs to be a "stable" relationship.* On one end of the continuum only two couples classified their relationship as casual. One couple had an "academic year" relationship. They lived together during the school year, dated others occasionally and planned to head in different directions for summer vacation. The other "casual"

---

*Each individual was asked to categorize their relationship. In those cases where couples did not similarly categorize their relationship I discussed the situation with the couple in order to decide which category most accurately described their relationship.

couple consisted of a female graduate student and a recent college graduate who worked for the university. They lived together at his place, but she also maintained her own apartment because they didn't always stay "together." On the other end of the continuum, only two couples classified their relationship as an alternative to marriage. In both of these cases the women were staunch feminists who viewed marriage as a degrading institution for women, and both stated they did not plan to have any children.

TABLE 25. CATEGORIZATION OF THEIR RELATIONSHIP

Description of Relationship	Absolute Frequency	Percentage
Casual	2	4
Transitory	16	32
Stable	19	38
Trial marriage	11	22
Alternative	2	4
	N=50	100%

The manner in which couples categorized their relationship is correlated with the length of time that they have been together. The longer that the couple has been living together the more likely they are to categorize their relationship as more permanent in nature. Of those who categorized their relationship as an "alternative to marriage," 100 percent have been living together more than one year. Of those who categorized their relationship as a trial marriage, 64 percent have been together at least one year. Among the group who categorized their relationship as "stable," 42 percent have been living together for more than a year. However only 25 percent of those who consider their relationship "transitory" have been together for that long a period of time. Finally, 50 percent of those who are maintaining a "casual" relationship have been together as long as one year. Table 26 summarizes these findings.

TABLE 26. TYPE OF RELATIONSHIP BY LENGTH OF TIME
COUPLE HAS BEEN COHABITING

Type of Relationship	Cohabiting At Least 1 Year	
Alternative	100%	(2 of 2)
Trial marriage	64%	(7 of 11)
Stable	42%	(8 of 19)
Transitory	25%	(4 of 16)
Casual	50%	(1 of 2)

The one casual couple that has maintained a relationship of just over one year does not spend all of their time staying together and does not expect to be together in the future.

The time that these couples had been involved with each other before they initiated a living-together relationship also appears to be correlated with the manner in which they categorized their relationship at the time of the interview.

TABLE 27. TYPE OF RELATIONSHIP BY DURATION OF INVOLVEMENT BEFORE COHABITATION

Type of Relationship	"Going Together" 7 Mos. or Longer Before Initiating Cohabitation
Alternative	100% (2 of 2)
Trial	56% (6 of 11)

60

TABLE 27 continued

Type of Relationship	"Going Together" 7 Mos. or Longer Before Initiating Cohabitation
Stable	79% (15 of 19)
Transitory	31% (5 of 16)
Casual	0% (0 of 2)

These findings together with data gathered in the interviews suggest that both length of time together before cohabitation and length of time cohabiting are correlated with the couple's categorization of their relationship. Furthermore, the process of living together clearly allows time to redefine the relationship; the longer they live together the more likely they are to define their relationship as permanent.

Plans for the Future

Perhaps the most interesting area of the findings to explore is that of evaluating how these couples feel about the future of their relationship. Do they plan to eventually marry the person with whom they are living? Do they expect to stay together? Table 28 details the future plans of the couples in the sample according to the manner in which they categorized their relationship.

Since the definitions of the various categories describing the relationship include, in part, plans for the future, we would expect to find some correlation between the type of relationship of the couple and their plans for the future. This certainly appears to be true for this sample. At one end of the continuum we find that both "casual" couples are not planning to be together in the future. Both of these couples stated that they are separating at least for the summer. One member of each of these couples will be traveling while the other is working. In one case both partners explained that they did think they would be getting back together. The other couple stated that they did not really even know where they would be individually when the summer ends and, therefore, could not make any plans to be together. At the other end of the continuum both couples classified as alternative definitely planned to be together.

Examination of the future plans for "transitory," "stable," and "trial marriage" couples reveals what might be expected from their definitions. None of the transitory couples expected to be married; about one-third of the stable couples thought their future included marriage (to each other) and 82 percent, or 9 of 11 of the trial marriage couples, expected to be married.

If we dichotomize the data for future plans by combining the marriage and definitely stay together categories, the data produces the statistics shown in Table 29. This table differentiates between those couples who feel certain of a continuing relationship and those who express at least some doubt as to what will happen. The data reveals that approximately half (26) of the couples definitely plan to stay together while the other half (24 couples) are al least somewhat doubtful about their future.

Difficulties and Disagreements

In considering unmarried cohabiting relationships it is now appropriate to look at the areas of difficulties and disagreement.

Description of the Relationship

Plans for the Future of the Relationship	Casual	Trans-itory	Stable	Trial Marriage	Alter-native	Total
Marriage	(0)	(0)	(6) 32%	(9) 82%	(0)	(15)
Definitely stay together	(0)	(1) 6%	(8) 42%	(0)	(2) 100%	(11)
Probably stay together	(0)	(6) 38%	(4) 21%	(2) 18%	(0)	(12)
Vague	(0)	(9) 56%	(1) 5%	(0)	(0)	(10)
Split	(2) 100%	(0)	(0)	(0)	(0)	(2)
	(2) 100%	(16) 100%	(19) 100%	(11) 100%	(2) 100%	(50)

TABLE 29. FUTURE PLANS BY TYPE OF RELATIONSHIP

Type of Relationship

Future Plans	Casual	Trans-itory	Stable	Trial Marriage	Alter-native	Total
Marriage	(0)	(1) 6%	(14) 74%	(9) 82%	(2) 100%	(26) 52%
Definitely stay together						
Probably stay together	(2) 100%	(15) 94%	(5) 26%	(2) 18%	(0)	(24) 48%
Vague						
Split						

In this section I present some topics which lead to disagreement between partners and evaluate both the difficulties anticipated and those actually encountered.

I asked couples to define for me the topics or issues that lead to disagreements. Although this was an open-ended question (i.e., I did not suggest topics or issues), 82 percent of the couples mentioned at least one area or topic on which they were not in agreement. In the interview I asked, "What are the areas in which you and your partner disagree?" and "How do you resolve these differences?" In the discussion which follows I will present information obtained both from the questionnaire and the interview. The range of topics on which couples experienced disagreements included marriage, the future of their relationship, commitment, jealousy, sexual fidelity, money, religion, drugs or drinking, abortion, and politics.

Marriage

Ten percent (five couples) revealed that the major topic about which they had disagreements was marriage. In four of the five cases the female stated that she would prefer it if they were married. The male partner in three of these cases stated in some form either that he wanted to wait or was not prepared to make a decision at the time. In the fourth situation Larry explained that he felt no need for a marriage contract.

We have a marital relationship without the psychological 'ties' of marriage....Marriage (that is legal marriage) is completely unnecessary and there should be no reason for the state to be concerned with private relationships.

His partner, however, felt differently stating that, "I see no reason not to get married since it would make life easier (financially and relations with parents) but he doesn't want to get married yet." Often the discussion of marriage is inextricably intertwined with other areas such as relationships with parents, religion, abortion, etc. Although marriage specifically may not be the topic, an additional seven couples stated that the "future" of their relationship is often an area of conflict. As one male respondent put it, "Sometimes we question whether we can grow as much together as we might apart." A female member of one couple explained, "At first we argued about marriage, now about some aspects of women's liberation, sometimes money and sometimes how much we really want to stay together." Finally, another female respondent indicated that their future as a couple was in conflict with their individual career goals--"It looks like his plans for the future may be in conflict with mine. I don't know if we can work it out."

Commitment, Jealousy, Sexual Fidelity

In the following analysis I do not mean to imply that cohabitation is the only type of relationship in which questions of overinvolvement, commitment, jealousy, etc. can produce problems. Rather I suggest that the very nature of cohabitation produces a situation in which participants are particularly susceptible to these problems. Due to the precarious nature of the relationship the testing of compatability and the question of level of involvement, cohabitants are potentially less secure than either in marriage or in a "dating" situation. In the marriage relationship a supposedly permanent commitment has already been made and in the more casual dating situation the reduced level of involvement lessens the potential fear of loss of love in the relationship.

Cohabiting couples must deal with a number of problems related to the level of commitment and involvement, especially with respect to outside heterosexual friend-

63

ships. As McCall has pointed out and my data supports, there is somewhat of a paradox in the new pattern of couple relationships. Marriage has become less exclusive and permanent, but in what used to be the courtship stage there is an emphasis on deep personal intimacy and commitment. (McCall, 1966:190-200)

Cohabitors often find themselves in a situation where it is difficult to balance a number of personal objectives. They want their relationships to be secure and protected and yet they are somewhat fearful of becoming overinvolved and dependent. According to Mackline (1974:30)

One is tempted to hypothesize that how one deals with the problem of overdependency and subsequent jealousy and feeling of entrapment may well be one of the major issues facing cohabiting couples. As in marriage, achieving security without giving up the freedom to be oneself, and growing together while leaving enough space so that the individuals may also grow, may well be central to the success in the relationship.

Interviews with respondents indicate that the problem of commitment is related both to stage of life and to the lack of clearly defined accepted rules of conduct in a relationship. As transadults (youth) they are fearful of cutting off new areas of experience, yet as a partner in a cohabiting relationship they feel the need for a certain degree of security and faithfulness in the relationship. Just as there is no clearly defined and acceptable sexual ethic (Reiss, 1960; Bell, 1966) there are apparently no clearly defined and acceptable rules among cohabitors governing the exclusivity of the relationships.

The area of sexual fidelity was mentioned as an issue which led to disagreements by five of the couples. When questioned about "rules or regulations" that the couple had set up either verbally or nonverbally, initially most stated they had none. However when asked specifically about sexual fidelity, some revealing aspect of contemporary cohabitation were brought out. An extremely typical response by one woman in the study when questioned concerning sexual fidelity in the relationship was,

When we first started living together, we agreed that if either of us wanted to date other people that was OK. We agreed to be honest about what we were doing and to tell the other person about it. Well, neither of us dated anyone for about three months, but then I met this guy in one of my classes and I told Rick that I though I wanted to go out with him. We just couldn't handle it. I went out a few times and so did he, but we found it caused hassles and we really didn't want to do it anyway.

My impression in the interview with this couple was that they had not as yet resolved the problem. Barbara wanted more freedom in the relationship but realized that when she followed through on their verbal commitment to allow outside relationships it caused great conflict in her relationship with her partner. Rich, though reluctant to admit his jealousy, stated that when Barbara was "going out" he felt obligated to find someone else. They temporarily resolved the problem by agreeing not to "date" others until they had established a firmer bond between each other that could not be jeopardized by relationships with others. Although unmarried cohabitants often profess an idelogy of freedom to do what they want individually and the "ridiculousness" of jealousy, it appears that they often fall prey to that particular evil. Although some couples forthrightly reject the idea of "dating" or being with others, most state that each partner is free to do as he or she pleases. More often when the ideal becomes reality, and when one partner does "go out," problems in the relationship arise. The most frequently encountered situation is when both partners say they can date others from within the security of the fact that neither actually does.

Finances

I have already discussed some of the financial aspects of the cohabiting couple. They, like married couples, often have disagreements concerning monetary matters. Six couples, or twelve percent of those sampled, stated that money was the major topic about which they were most likely to disagree. In some cases one partner is much better off financially and feels he or she is not being treated fairly when paying a larger of expenses. Helen explained that problems concerning money, in her relationship with Frank, came from two sources. She feels that Frank has failed to live up to the bargain they had made with respect to household responsibilities; and the fact that she contributed more financially than he did made the situation even worse. According to Helen.

Our arguments are almost always about money. The way it usually comes up is when it's his turn to cook. He hates to cook but he agreed that he would do it about half the time. Well, it seems like whenever it's his turn to cook he wants to use 'our' money to go out to eat. It just doesn't make sense to me. He usually wants to spend more than I think we should. It's not that I'm so cheap its just that we don't have it to waste and it gets me angry because I bring in most of the money from my waitress job."

In other cases the arguments stem from disagreements over how the money should be spent. For example, as one respondent stated, "Nancy wants us to use all our savings to go to Europe this summer. I think we should work so we don't have to during the year." Nancy argued it was "their last chance" to get away while Bob took what he called a more reasonable position. Although money was not a major topic of disagreement for most of the couples, it was often mentioned as an area that occasionally caused heated discussion.

Religion

In the section outlining the background characteristics of the respondents I indicated that in this sample the majority of the couples did not come from similar religious backgrounds. The relatively low frequency in which religion is mentioned as a topic of disharmony is quite interesting. In fact only three couples stated that religion was a major area of disagreement. The frequency seems surprisingly low in as much as sixty percent of the couples in the sample differ in their religious background.

In two cases the disagreement between the partners concerned the concept of God. In one case the male was Protestant and the female listed herself as an agnostic. In the other case the situation was reversed, the female was Protestant and the male categorized himself as an agnostic. In the final case the argument between the couple concerned the topic of conversion. In that case the male was Jewish and the female stated that neither she nor her parents had any institutionalized religious affiliation. This couple had been cohabiting for more than a year and planned to be married. The male's parents wanted them to be married by a rabbi in a conservative temple and asked that his partner convert to Judaism. The female insisted that though she did want to be married, she felt it would be too dishonest to convert since she had no "religious" orientation or desire to be affiliated with any religious sect. This couple had not yet resolved this difference of opinion but did plan to marry in the near future.

It is interesting to note that the data suggest a possible correlation between similarity of religious background and plans for the future. The two-by-two table below suggests a relationship between plans to be married and similarity of religious background.

TABLE 30. SIMILARITY OF RELIGIOUS BACKGROUND AND PLANS TO BE MARRIED IN THE NEAR FUTURE

Future Plans	Similar Religious Affiliation	Mixed Religious Background	Total
Plans marriage in near future	(8) 40%	(7) 23%	30%
Does not plan to be married in near future	(12) 60%	(23) 77%	70%
	N=50 100%	N=30 100%	100%

Drugs and Alcohol

A sixth topic area mentioned by couples as their major disagreement was the abuse of drugs or alcohol. In the three cases in which this topic was mentioned the female member of the couple indicated that she felt her partner overindulged in either smoking, drug usage or drinking. As Fran said, "We often fight about habits (i.e., drinking and smoking grass and cigarettes). My partner partakes and I don't." Kathy stated that Bob has a tendency to waste too much of his time being high.

Sometimes I want to go out and do things, see our friends or visit relatives. Lots of times all he wants to do is stay home and get high. It's a real problem for me because I really don't like to go alone, but it's hard to get him to do things and I think it's because he smokes too much.

Finally, Joe and Joan indicated they argued most about Joe's drinking. He explained that when he gets angry or upset he just likes to do some drinking and forget his troubles. Joan complained that when this happens he also gets nasty sometimes and she says she just doesn't know how to relate to him when he's like that. All three of these couples are planning to be married, and my impression, from the interviews, was that the women wanted to resolve the problems before marriage. However, in only one case did the male partner feel that he sould work on changing his behavior. Joe admitted his drinking was not the best way to handle being upset, but he was not sure he could change. Bob did not think his getting high was a problem; "We just enjoy different types of recreation." Steve, Fran's partner, explained, "She worries too much. I really don't smoke much at all, it's just cause she doesn't that it seems like a problem to her."

It was apparent that on the topic of drugs most couples do agree and this agreement usually means that they agree to moderate use of illegal drugs. Among those few couples who did not use drugs there was agreement between the partners not to indulge. In the vast majority of the cases in which respondents indicated use of drugs they often confined themselves to the use of "grass." A few occasionally used LSD, speed or tranquilizers. Of those who do use drugs, approximately half (20 couples) said they smoked frequently (i.e., three times a week or more). Again, this use of drugs was almost exclusively marijuana.

Abortions

Another area that was described as a topic of disagreement is what to do in case of pregnancy. Most couples are clearly in agreement about what should be done. Table 31 indicates the couples' response to the question, "If you found you were expecting a child, what would you do?"

TABLE 31. RESPONSE TO AN UNEXPECTED PREGNANCY

Response	Absolute Frequency	Percentage
Abortion	33	66
Marriage	6	12
Have child without marriage	1	2
Don't know (use protection)	8	16
Disagree	2	4
	N=50	100%

As can be seen from this table most couples felt abortion was the appropriate response. Six couples said that although they didn't plan to have children at the time, they would marry if a pregnancy occurred. Only one couple agreed that they would keep the child and not get married. Some (8 couples) stated frankly that they didn't know what they would do. Two of the women in this group stated they would want to have the child but would not unless their partner agreed. Although they were unsure what they would do, they did not feel this was an important area of disagreement.* Finally, two couples pointed out that this was a topic on which they had not been able to agree.

In one case the couple revealed that they had often discussed this issue, especially since she was using a diaphragm and "once in a while" they did have sex without taking the proper precautions. Lorraine stated that she did not think that she would be capable of having an abortion if she got pregnant. Her partner, however, felt that they were not realistically able to handle a child at this time. In the interview they could not offer a good explanation as to why they were not more careful, especially since they could not agree as to how they would handle the situation if she did become pregnant.

In the other case the male thought abortion would be absolutely wrong. He saw himself as a naturalist, refused to use drugs of any sort. "I believe all drugs are harmful and unnecessary even if dispensed by a doctor." He did not believe in disturbing, as he put it, "the natural process." He had acquiesced in terms of agreeing that his partner use a diaphragm as a birth control mechanism, but he was totally against the idea of abortion if she should become pregnant. On the other hand, his partner stated emphatically that she would not even consider having a child now even if they got married. As she put it, "I just couldn't deal with a child at this point; I'm not ready not matter what Mickey thinks."

Politics

A final area of disagreement can perhaps best be categorized under the general topic of politics. This category includes disagreements concerning women's liberation, level of political activism and political ideology. Four couples in the sample revealed that political questions are likely to be the topic when they find themselves in a real disagreement. For two of these couples the relationship seemed to be particularly one sided. In the first couple (Tom and Laura) Laura apparently was the

---

*All the couples in the sample were practicing some form of birth control including the pill, diaphragm or IUD.

dominant partner. She seemed to be the decision maker, held stronger views on all issues, and apparently felt less need for the security of the relationship. Laura described herself as a feminist, claimed she would never consider getting involved in an oppresive institution such as marriage, and did not plan to have children. She explained to me in the interview that she and Tom share the same political ideology based on fighting for women's liberation, gay liberation and in favor of most "radical" causes. Tom's comment on this issue in his part of the interview was that he did not particularly agree with any one ideology or doctrine. The area of disagreement centered around the level of political participation in causes. Laura wanted involvement and action; Tom seemed more concerned with dealing with his own day-to-day problems.

A second couple in which level of activism seemed to create difficulties was John and Julie. In this case it was John who saw himself as a radical and a fighter. He is angry at the oppression he sees around him and does not feel the world is a fit place for children. He has worked in political "struggles" and sees that not enough is being done. He feels that in the relationship as well they must fight against the sins of possessiveness and jealousy. He would like to form a loving-sharing cooperative. Julie, on the other hand, is not interested in acting on an ideology; she states she believes in but cannot quite cope with herself. As she put it, "I can love and respect and show concern for all people, but I don't want to share my life with everyone." While John wants to fight for new life styles and the new left, Julie seems to prefer watching from the sidelines.

Bob and Lori are on the same political wave length. She works hard at the women's center, on political newspapers, and at the free clinic. He devotes much time and energy to the tenant's union, workers strikes, and organizing young factory workers trying to "get them involved in the political process." According to Bob abd Lori their problem is that their politics gets in the way of their personal lives. They get angry at themselves and with each other when they can not get enough done or do what has to be done as well as they would like.

The final couple who found their disagreements center on "political" issues was John and Stephanie. John's age, twenty-five, is five years older than his partner and he explained that part of the problem is that it's hard for him to accept some of the changes that are taking place. He was one of only two respondents in the sample to classify himself as a Republican. In response to the question concerning topics of disagreement he said, "...most recently women's liberation. I guess I still have a way to go to realize how she feels about certain areas of womanhood." For her part Stephanie explained that he sometimes gets upset by her friends, "They like to get high and have a looser attitude about relationships." John seems to have trouble allowing Stephanie to function on hew own and this is the main source of friction in their relationship.

As a means of summarizing the information concerned with "disagreements," the data is presented in Table 32 below:

TABLE 32. MAJOR TOPIC WHICH LEADS TO DISAGREEMENT

Topic or Issue	Absolute Frequency	Percentage
Marriage or future of relationship	12	24
Sexual fidelity	5	10
Money	6	12
Religion	3	6
Drugs or drink	3	6
Abortion	2	4
Politics	4	8
No particular topic	6	12
None	9	18
	N=50	100%

68

In response to a question asking whether cohabitation involved more or less difficulties than expected, more than half the couples said they had fewer difficulties than expected in "living together." Lynn explained she was pleasantly surprised, "I thought there would be more problems and interference with my separate life (school, friends, etc.). I also somehow expected more fights." A male respondent couldn't believe it could be so trouble free, "After the last person I lived with, there is amazement in my heart and head that it is so easy to get along with another person." On the other hand, approximately twenty percent said they actually "had more difficulty working out personal differences than I thought we would, especially learning to say 'I'm wrong' and 'I'm sorry'." One female put it this way: "I guess I never thought about difficulties before we were living together. When the difficulties came they hurt like hell."

Although cohabitants are aware of the problems of cohabitation, the question of overinvolvement, jealousy, limits on freedom, obligations, problems with parents, legal hassles, and the precarious nature of the relationship, they are quick to point out that the advantages far outweigh the disadvantages.

Advantages

One should not be midled by the many difficulties or problems referred to for those in cohabiting relationships. The great majority of cohabitants evaluated their relationships quite positively. As I talked with respondents, they referred to the great many advantages of the cohabiting relationship. Their positive comments ranged from companionship and emotional satisfaction to the financial practicality of the arrangement. They often mentioned their own individual growth as well as the advantages of the couple relationship. As one male cohabitant put it,

I've learned how to relate to another person and I've learned a
lot about myself. I think I'm more considerate and understanding
than I was before. You know living in a dormitory or a fraternity
house with a bunch of young guys may not be the best way to develop
as a human being.

The single most often mentioned benefit of cohabitation was the companionship and sharing that it offered. Again and again respondents indicated that life on a large university campus, though filled with studies, activities and people, can be a lonely place. They stressed that cohabitation offers a growing sense of intimacy, an opportunity to drop your guard, to be with another person. The closeness and intensity of the cohabiting relationship, according to respondents, also offers a situation in which one can be at ease, totally informal, and relaxed. The opportunity to develop an intimate relationship with another human being in which each could share with the other their deepest personal thoughts and feelings. It is interesting to note that many clearly indicated that the lack of permanent bond or commitment did not inhibit the relationship from fulfilling these companionship needs. The cohabiting situation is an experience in which the individual gains knowledge of how to relate to another person on an intimate level as well as an opportunity to learn about the opposite sex.

Many respondents mentioned the sexual advantages of cohabitation which included: a readily available partner, the increased opportunity to integrate the personal and sexual aspects of one's life, and the decrease in the tension in this aspect of the relationship. Many indicated that their sexual lives together had improved a great deal since they started cohabiting. As one respondent explained, "Now that we live together we are much more at ease with each other. The tension created by making love and then leaving to go home was driving us both nuts."

Some respondents pointed out that they felt cohabitation was a means of developing more egalitarian relationships. Since cohabitors are not married, and in most cases have not made a permanent commitment to each other, some felt that they were more likely to maintain a partnership-type relationship. They argue that in traditional marriage the man takes on the role of provider and the woman that of housewife. Although the data indicates that many of these couples did divide household chores according to traditional sex role patterns, some were constantly aware of and maintained an equal division of labor in the household. Even for those who fell into sterotypical sex roles in terms of domestic activities, the vast majority maintained an equal sharing concerning financial obligations. The area of finances, in fact, not only represented an advantage with respect to egalitarianism, but cohabitation was almost universally perceived as more economical. According to respondents, though two may not be able to live as cheaply as one, they were sure that they lived more economically than two single individuals.

Earlier I quoted a young man who explained that his parents thought his cohabitation was a very good idea. He said,

My parents think Janet is terrific. I think they like her better
than me. My father always thought I was a bum but now he knows
I'm doing better in school, eating better, using less drugs and
having a far more stable existence.

A number of respondents indicated that along with cohabitation they found themselves leading a somewhat more responsible existence. Instead of eating TV dinners and hamburgers they were eating home cooked meals. Instead of, as Russell suggested, going to "parties and orgies" they were staying home and studying. Some indicated that moving out of a dorm or fraternity house represented a growing sense of responsibility and maturity. Now they had to pay their own bills, buy their own food, take out their own garbage. Others stated that this really was the first time they had to take care of themselves. In some cases those initiating a living-together relationship felt they no longer had the right to ask parents to support them. One could argue that either marriage or living on one's own would bring about this same growth or maturity and responsibility. However, in the example above, Steve had been living on his own before meeting Janet and neither he nor Janet felt ready for marriage. For both of them, as well as for other cohabitants, an advantage of their living arrangement was a feeling of stability and development of a sense of responsibility.

Finally, a clearly stated advantage seen by many is the opportunity to experience a trial marriage. The chance to clarify one's needs, desires, and expectations in a relationship as well as their inadequacies. Most felt that living together provided the best possible means of getting to know a prospective marriage partner and testing their compatability as a couple. Some couples felt cohabitation was a good testing ground, others felt it was a means of learning what they might or might not want in a future relationship. In either case they saw the experience as an important benefit of the cohabitation relationship.

Cohabitants spoke of companionship, learning about themselves, each other, growing together, responsibility, as well as the economy of the arrangement, and the sexual advantages. They said that they loved each other and wanted to be together as much as possible. Obviously cohabitation maximizes the opportunity.

Attitudes Toward Cohabitation and Marriage

In this final section on findings I report respondents attitudes concerning cohabitation as a permanent "alternative" to marriage, the possibility of having children in a relationship without marriage, their attitudes toward the need to promote change in legal relationships, and their feelings on legalized cohabitation and other alternative forms.

It is clear that in only a small minority of cases do couples view their relationship as a permanent "alternative" to marriage. Most state that they do plan to marry eventually and many point out that marriage can be one of the goals of a cohabiting relationship. Over 75 percent of the respondents indicated that they felt cohabitation was helpful in making the "right choice" for marriage.

In answer to the question, "Do you think you will eventually marry the person you are living with?" 54 percent of the males and 56 percent of the females said they did expect to marry their cohabitation partner at some point. Furthermore, the responses to the question, "Do you think you will eventually marry anyone?" offers an interesting insight into the phenomenon of cohabitation. Only 3 of the 50 males and only 4 of the 50 females stated that they did not expect to ever get married. Combining a number of findings, the data reveals that 30 percent of the couples are planning to be married in the forseeable future. An additional 20 percent think they may eventually marry the person with whom they are now cohabiting, yet only a very small percentage of the sample entirely rejects the concept of institutionalized marriage. Therefore, even for those who do not view their immediate cohabitation as a prelude to marriage (except in a very few cases), they are not seeking to remain unmarried indefinitely.

In answer to a general question as to whether unmarried cohabitants should have children, approximately 40 percent gave a definite No response, and approximately 20 percent answered positively. However, an additional 34 percent of the males and over 40 percent of the females stated that under certain conditions it would be "right" to have children. Among this group a number of explanatory comments can be instructive. A typical comment frequently made was,

I think unmarried couples should have children if they want them,
but they have to consider if the society around them could accept
it. They also have to be responsible enough to make sure kids are
well taken care of.

Another respondent stated, "If we were to stay right here I don't think it would be difficult; all our friends and neighbors know our situation and in a university community it probably would not cause much excitement." Table 33 reports the responses to the general question. "Do you think that unmarried couples should have children?"

TABLE 33. SHOULD UNMARRIED COUPLES HAVE CHILDREN (by Sex)

Response	Male	Female	Total
No	40%	42%	41%
Yes	26	42	38
Yes (Conditional)	34	16	21
	100%	100%	100%

(N=50)

When asked specifically whether they themselves would consider having children without marriage, the answer was overwhelmingly No. As one member of a couple put it, "We certainly aren't ready for kids now and if we ever are we'll get married first. Kids have enough problems as it is." Most agreed that it would be unfair, or at least difficult, for children; therefore they themselves would not consider having children without marriage. Two couples stated that they never expected to have children, while a number of other couples explained that they had serious doubts about whether they would have children even if they were married.

When asked whether they were working in any way to seek reforms in the laws concerning legal relationships, their responses indicated that "cohabitors" do not possess a group identification. Cohabitors do not view their behavior as radical, and not one of the respondents in the sample belonged to any organization devoted to developing alternative family arrangements or changes in existing legal statutes. However, most argue that our marriage and divorce laws are in dire need of reform. Their comments were most often related to the easing of regulations concerning divorce. Almost ninety percent of the respondents felt that divorce should be easier to accomplish. Most felt that it should be at least as easy as marriage. They do not feel the need to work politically either in the system or outside it to change these laws. As a group they do not identify themselves as "unmarried couples," "cohabitors," or "deviates" and do not feel descrimitated against. The only "legal" complaint they had as a group was the difficulty in obtaining residences. Living together, i.e., cohabitation, is illegal and some landlords are unwilling to rent to cohabiting couples. As a group there is no movement to gain legal status for their relationship.

In my discussions with cohabitants I asked if they would be interested in legal alternative forms. I explained that a number of "legal" alternatives had been suggested ranging from registering the fact of living together, to trial marriage contracts, to marriage contracts for people who do not plan to have children, to renewable marriages. (Bernard, 1972) The most typical immediate reaction to suggestions of legalized living together was, as one respondent put it, "Why be bothered with any legal mechanisms? No one is being prosecuted for living together; it just means more problems." However, many of the respondents, after giving more thought to the possible implications of a legalized contract suggested situations in which legalization or institutionalization of cohabitation may be advantageous. It was pointed out that some forms of legalization may be helpful in reducing friction with parents and relatives, that tax benefits may be available and legal contracts such as leases, loans, etc., would probably present fewer problems.

Carrying the question somewhat further I asked respondents if they thought legal alternatives such as trial marriage or renewable contracts would be available in the near future, and if these were available to them whether they themselves would be interested in a legalized version of their relationship. Most respondents indicated that they felt legal alternatives should and would be available in the future for those who wanted them or felt they needed them. They often commented that laws prohibiting cohabitation are not usually enforced and should be stricken from the books for consenting adults (i.e., those of age 18 or older). When asked if they specifically would be interested in legalizing their relationships in some form other than traditional marriage, more than half indicated that they would not have any interest in a legal stamp of approval. However, over forty percent did reveal some interest in certifying their relationship in some manner. In fact half of the females and forty-two percent of the males in the sample indicated at least some interest in establishing some legal basis for their relationship. As one young woman said,

If I could show my parents some legal piece of paper that says
it's OK for me to screw, it would make things a lot easier. It
really wouldn't make any difference to me, but that's where their
heads are at so I'd do it for them.

Although most did not put it as bluntly as she did, many indicated that their reasons for wanting legal alternatives usually focused on others rather than themselves. A male respondent stated,

My parents make me feel guilty about ruining Judy's life--they
think I should marry her or leave her. If there was a sort of
half way step that didn't involve a permanent commitment we
might both be interested just to ease the tension but I don't
know if that kind of thing would be better or just increase

the pressure to get really married.
Although some focused on the easing of tension with parents, others indicated that a legal contract would be most valuable in terms of dealing with landlords, banks and taxes. One couple related,

We have this thing about honesty and when we went looking for an
apartment we didn't want to sign a lease Mr. and Mrs., but twice
we lost apartments because of it. Finally Brad got the apartment
in his own name and I just moved in with him. If we could have
said something like we are a legally registered cohabiting couple
there might have been less hassle. Isn't it ridiculous.

Finally, a small group of respondents thought that a legal alternative would be very valuable, particularly a "no children" contract that could be dissolved by either party at any time. The freedom, according to these people, would be there but the legal contract could eliminate some of the hardships of cohabitation.

As a final aspect of evaluating their relationship I discussed with many of the respondents what they would consider the ideal living situation. I was interested in exploring respondents' attitudes concerning group marriage, communal living, cooperatives, and marriage generally. Clearly the respondents in this sample do not condemn the institution of marriage. As I pointed out, almost all expect to marry someone at some time in the future, if not necessarily the person with whom they are living. They do, however, see marriage as a somewhat confining and restrictive institution with males slightly more likely to condemn marriage than females.

The most frequently mentioned advantage of marriage is the reduction of stigma and the relieving of tension in relationships with parents and other relatives. Other factors mentioned as advantages included less "legal" hassles (leases, loans, taxes, etc.) and a more secure atmosphere in which to have children. As one fellow put it, "It's acceptable and tax deductible."

In answer to the question of other alternatives, the majority of the group was not particularly interested in either group marriages or communal living. A few suggested that they would like to try living with another couple where all four could "love" each other in a deep and meaningful way. They were keenly aware, however, of their need for privacy and of the difficulty of finding two other people who they both could love and who would also love them.

Many, however, did express some interest in what might loosely be called cooperative living arrangements. Most saw suburban middle-class life as isolated and alienating. They seem to be interested in expanding their relationships beyond the nuclear family and seeking at least some aspects of "communal life." They suggested that we really need more than one adult to relate to and that children can benefit also with more adult role models. Although most had only sketchy ideas as to how they might achieve their goals, a pattern of desires can be detailed.

Unlike the type of commune that isolates itself from society, the picture they drew seems to include a small collection (two, three or four families) which will interact in a cooperative fashion with each other and the outside society. They speak of a kind of physical proximity that would allow for a sharing of tasks and responsibilities. We know, for instance, that neighbors will occasionally work together on a July 4th picnic or a Labor Day barbecue. The theme they seemed to be outlining takes this concept somewhat further. Though many different suggestions were made, a central focus emerged which I present here only as a very tentative conglomeration of the concepts which were suggested in a number of group interviews. Many envisioned some form or other of a multi-family house in which each family would have its own area. However "communal" or "cooperative" rooms would also be available. As an example there might be only one clothes washer and dryer, communal TV and recreation rooms and one swimming pool, etc. They spoke very much, in fact, like the fictional couples in Robert Rimmer's Proposition 31 and listed such advantages as economy, availability of baby sitters, ability for parents, particularly mothers, to cooperate in performing child-caring responsibilities or hire professionals so that the women would be more free to follow careers. A single factor that continually emerged in these discussions was that adults in this setting would benefit by having a variety of other adults to interact with and that they would also provide a wider variety of role models for the children. Without going much farther into these concepts it is apparent that at least some of these young people are seeking alternatives to the single nuclear family in the suburbs. They claim to be interested in developing a spirit of community to combat the bureaucracy and the technology that they see creating an isolated, nonemotional, noninteractive world around them.

CHAPTER V

IMPLICATIONS FOR THE FUTURE

This final chapter examines the proposition that cohabitation among unmarried middle-class youth, though a recent social phenomenon, has become quasi-institutionalized. Most participants view their behavior as normative and acceptable, particularly within the academic environment. I will discuss the apparent acceptance of a coneptual model of courtship proposed by Lindsey and Russell, and later by Mead. Finally, I suggest the implications of cohabitation for courtship, marriage and the family.

Institutionalization

Martin Weinberg (1968) and Richard Stephenson (1973) discussed a number of stages through which the individual passes in order to involve himself in behavior formerly described as deviant or immoral. As Stephenson stated,

To engage in deviant behavior that violates prior patterns of socialization and normative standards of significant others requires, to some degree, a change in the definition of the situation that formerly guided or inhibited behavior. (Stephenson, 1973:173)

Both Weinberg's and Stephenson's analyses can be useful in examining the changes which took place in the environmental setting of the college campus and community which allowed unmarried heterosexual living together to be redefined as acceptable behavior. Although the analysis by Weinberg and Stephenson is directed more at group involvement situations (i.e., nudism and swinging), their theoretical approach does offer a framework within which we can examine the expansion and acceptance of cohabitation.

The first stage of resocialization or alteration of mores is described as a passive phase in which people are involved in learning, thinking and talking about a new mode of behavior or "deviant" activity. That is, the behavior must in some way become part of the realm of reality. One must know about the behavior and this behavior must involve "identifiable" and "acceptable" people. When knowledge of actual situations becomes public, particularly when participants do not suffer from the consequences of this public knowledge, the behavior becomes a more acceptable topic of discussion and it also gains an air of legitimacy. As I have described earlier, the latter sixties and early seventies saw a large number of newspaper articles and magazine stories concerning the living together phenomenon. The many articles, interviews with cohabiting couples, and publicity concerning college administration reaction to these situations, gave impetus to much discussion and raised consciousness concerning a behavior presumably considered to be deviant and not widely practiced. During this stage the credibility and feasibility of this type of behavior is further established. When the information being presented comes from respectable sources (The New York Times, Time, Newsweek, Saturday Review, etc.) and when participants are identified as acceptable (Barnard coed, Columbia junior) behavior formally "unthinkable" not only becomes thinkable but more likely to be discussed and rationalized.

In the active phase the discussion of "deviant" behavior leads to the possibility or potentiality of involvement in this behavior. As sexual standards and housing regulations were changing, the increase in overnight relationships became more plausible, and the sounding and testing of the active stage became more and more a part of the "dating-courtship" scene. The cohabiting couple is highly unlikely to start a cohabiting relationship the first time they sleep together. However, at this stage the couple can test out the relationship, spend the weekend together, a few days during the week and, according to the analysis employing the model of Weinberg and Stephenson, the possibility of involvement in the next stage emerges.

In the final phase, the behavior formerly perceived as deviant and unacceptable is rationalized and legitimized. Although some unmarried cohabitants do present themselves as being married under certain circumstances, the behavior itself in the final stage is considered as one among several alternative and acceptable "life styles" available in the general culture and particularly within the social structure and environment of the college campus community.

The college community of the late 1960's and early 1970's provided the environmental opportunity for the changing of norms and values related to geterosexual relationships. The alienation of the mid and late 60's led to a re-examination and reinterpretation of what would constitute acceptable premarital heterosexual behavior. The isolation of the college experience and the atmosphere of decreasing social control allowed for experimentation with new patterns of interaction. The technological advance and distribution of the pill virtually guaranteed "safe" sex, while the decreasing value of virginity and the increasing rights of women allowed greater freedom to develop sexually intimate relationships without strong feelings of guilt.

Finally, "acceptable" people were publicly acknowledging their involvement in cohabitation without serious consequences. The behavior was being talked about, discussed, and written about in the popular press. The college community in particular, with the demise of in loco parentis, gave tacit approval to and provided rationalizations for the acceptance of this "alternative" life style. Opportunity and potential for the formation of cohabiting relationships increased while social controls, both internal and external, were diminished.

It appears that over the past few years the phenomenon of cohabitation for middle-class, educated young people has evolved through the three stages suggested by Weinberg and Stephenson; that cohabitation formerly viewed as deviant has now become quite acceptable, at least within the college community environment. Others who have been studying this field have reached similar conclusions. In reviewing the status of cohabitation in 1974 Whitehurst stated:

> There is, however, a distinct air of legitimacy in the living
> together unmarried experimentation scene; it does not lend to
> the belief that it is revolutionary as behaviour. Rather, it
> is more likely to be seen as one of a slightly enlarged set of
> options in a slightly more pluralistic society that means more
> rational mate selection....It is not a kind of behaviour that
> elicits much praise or damnation from the press in 1974, nor is
> it even much of a curiosity. It is simply something lots of poeple
> do....Although frequencies of cohabitation have been variously
> reported on campuses ranging from about five to thirty percent,
> there are probably many campuses where cohabitation has passed
> the tip-point of fifty percent and thus it has become statistically
> normal if not legally normative. (Whitehurst, 1974:5; 1973:11)

Montgomery also suggests that there is likely to be continued growth of premarital cohabitation and that it is likely to become more acceptable. He supports the reasoning developed from the Weinberg and Stephenson perspective:

> Besides having social and subculture support, cohabitation
> serves to reinforce itself. The more cohabitation there is,

the more there will be. <u>It will be easier for people to do
simply because more people have done it.</u> (Montgomery, 1973:292, underline added)

Respondents indicate that they do not feel in any way chastised by their peers
for involving themselves in a cohabiting relationship. Furthermore, although some
parents and some landlords continue to frown on this type of behavior, participants
have a great deal of support from their friends. They define their behavior as
functioning within the norms for people who are in the transadult (youth) stage and
living in the university community.

Implications for Courtship, Marriage and the Family

In the first section of this chapter I indicated that a behavior formerly
viewed as deviant has progressed through a number of stages to the point that many
have accepted this behavior as normative. I pointed out that other researchers have
reached similar conclusions and that the respondents in this study support the
reasoning outlined above.

In this final section of the dissertation I recall the fact that schemes promot-
ing a pattern quite similar to that being adopted had been suggested as long as fifty
years ago, but that these ideas were rejected and their proponents were censured.
I then review the plan suggested by a more contemporary sociologist, indicate that
the major aspects of that conceptual model have become the reality without statutory
support, and finally suggest the potential implications of that reality for courtship,
marriage and the family.

A number of schemes suggesting arrangements whereby permanenet (parental) marriage would be viewed as a second step and that legal cohabitation would serve as a
testing ground for the relationship were reported in Chapter 1. As early as the
1920's Judge Lindsey proposed that engaged couples enter a prefatory stage of the
"companionate," before accepting the parental and other long range responsibilities
associated with legal marriage. Judge Lindsey's logic was indisputable. His facts
regarding the growth of unordered "trial sex" were substantially true. His indictment
of it was strong and moralistic. His plan was a rational instrument designed to ful-
fill a social need. Yet this renowned and socially minded jurist was severely criti-
cised. I also noted that Bertrand Russell, in 1929, supported premarital cohabitation
for college students suggesting that academic work and sex were more efficiently
combined in a heterosexual living together arrangement than in "the scramble and
excitement of parties and orgies." He maintained that it would be terribly unwise
to marry without premarital sexual experience and fuller knowledge of a potential mate.

It was reported that contemporary social thinkers have also proposed variations
in the traditional pattern of courtship and marriage. Margaret Mead's conception of
a two-step marriage was briefly outlined. The first step in Mead's scheme was very
similar to what Lindsey had called companionate marriage. The purpose of the initial
stage (individual marriage) was to give the two partners a chance to really get to
know each other in order to find out whether they are compatible and desire to go
to the more serious and "hopefully" more permanent commitment of having a child together (parental marriage). Mead envisioned students and young people (transadults)
as the prime participants in individual marriage. Her argument was that young people
on the one hand need the opportunity to experience intimacy both sexually and per-
sonally. However, she maintained, on the other hand, that they are not ready nor
able to choose a partner for a lifetime commitment without greater knowledge of
their compatability. Thus the major objective of the individual marriage was for two
people to get to know each other. Mead suggested that, according to this scheme, if
the first step of the contract was not viewed as satisfactory the couple could part

without great hardships. If, however, the individual marriage was found to be successful then the couple can more confidently decide they wich to go on to step two, parental marriage, and have children. Mead did not rule out divorce in the parental marriage, but agreed that this should be more difficult to achieve than in the individual marriage. The expectation would be that parental marriage would be a lifetime commitment.

As the research for this dissertation and other projects has pointed out, something resembling the scheme proposed by Mead in the mid 60's has come to be a rather familiar pattern among middle-class, educated individuals without the legal accompaniment of a formal contract. Obviously many young people in their twenties, particularly those who have gone to residential colleges, have been and continue to be involved in cohabitation relationships.

One difference between the schemes suggested by Lindsey and Mead and the phenomenon of contemporary cohabitation is the level of commitment necessary before initiating a cohabiting relationship. Though Lindsey and Mead indicate that cohabitation be reserved for "engaged" couples, today's cohabitors do not necessarily view their cohabitation as an engagement period or preparation for "parental" marriage. It is clear that the vast majority perceive a difference between cohabitation and marriage. However, although some cohabitation is defined as a convenienve relationship, and others see their cohabitation as a permanent alternative, much of it can be described as a testing of the compatability of the relationship, a means of getting to know a potential marital partner as completely as possible (though they are reluctant to classify their relationship as a "trial marriage"). It is also apparent that cohabitors do not reject the concept of marriage and are likely to expect to be married in the future. Though they may or may not plan to marry the person with whom they are cohabiting, respondents generally do retain the image of marriage as a permanent commitment. In fact many of the respondents indicated that they would not even consider marrying without the benefit of a trial period in which to assess the relationship. They clearly believe that living together will help them in making the right choice for marriage, and they do consider it a rational approach to the difficult task of finding a mate.

The most widely reprinted article on cohabitation was written by Eleanor D. Macklin and appeared in the Family Coordinator in October of 1972. In discussing the possible implications of cohabitation she stated the following:

It appears that cohabitation has become an increasingly common aspect of courtship on the campus studied and one could predict that the trend will proliferate....The pattern which is currently evolving appears to be primarily concerned with total relationships and only incidentally with the sexual aspects. It is this concern with getting to know another as a whole person and the emphasis on sharing as openly and as completely as possible with that person, which is probably the major new dimension being added to old courtship patterns. (Macklin, 1972, underline added)

Montgomery discussing his assesment of modern courtship states:

....Courtship, in past years, consisted of a progressive limiting of partners until the person found the one that was best for him. Marriage then took place with the person who had been selected. Contemporary courtship is more of a series of intense relationships which last as long as the needs of the individuals are being met. The decision to marry takes place when one of the relationships lasts long enough to include it. (Montgomery, 1973:270)

The data gathered for this dissertation supports the assessments of both Macklin and Montgomery as well as Farber and Reiss, that contemporary cohabitation is an extension of and reformulation of the institution of courtship. (Farber, 1964:168; Reiss, 1971:58-60)

As cohabitation becomes the norm, as I and others suggest it will (or has), we should consider the role of cohabitation in the courtship process. Although marriage historically was the end point of a series of stages--dating, going steady, agreement to marry, formal engagement, and then marriage--the evidence suggests that the structure of the institution of courtship has changed. Whereas in the past, courtship could be described as the narrowing of the field of eligibles and increasing commitment, it has evolved to a series of "relationships," one of which may result in marriage.

Over thirty percent of young people in this sample have cohabited with someone else prior to this relationship. Although males were more likely to have had more partners than females, about an equal number of males (34 percent) and females (28 percent) have had experience with heterosexual living together in the past. Furthermore, among the fifteen couples who stated they plan to be married, six couples included at least one partner who had been involved in a former cohabiting relationship that did not end in marriage (of course it is quite possible that not all those couples considering marriage will in fact marry, thus adding to the proportion of those who experience cohabitation that does not result in marriage).

If we view cohabitation as a rational extension of the courtship process, the suggested restructuring of the continuum would include: dating (initial stages of relationship); going steady (spending time together on a regular bases); cohabiting; agreement to move on to the legal establishment of the relationship; marriage.

The apparent trend is toward testing out a number of relationships through the third stage and then to enter a legal marriage relationship. This process would tend to support the delaying of marriage perhaps, even until the decision to have children (parental marriage).

Many researchers have posed the question as to what the impact of cohabitation will be on marriage. Unfortunately, though research has helped define the questions, we have not yet been able to gather the data that will supply tbe answers to these questions. Longitudinal research will be necessary of we are to effectively analyze the impact of cohabitation; yet defining the areas of concern is a prerequisite to this research. Some major questions are: Will cohabitation with its increased potential for more complete knowledge of the potential mate and compatability of the dyad lead to more stable and enduring relationships? Or will the lack of permanent commitment in these relationships foster a holding back of emotional involvement and commitment? Will the easy accessability of a marital-like situation diminish the desire for contractual arrangement? Will cohabitation with its ideology of equality and sharing, openness and espoused lack of exclivsity become a more realistic part of cohabitation and, if so, will it carry over into marriage? Is the apparent acceptance of cohabitation in the educational community likely to carry over into the rest of the society and thereby effect marriage among youth who do not attend college?

At this point the one major theme on which nearly all those who have done research in the area agree is that cohabitation is closely associated with a delaying of marriage. (Whitehurst, 1973; Danziger and Greenwald, 1973; Macklin, 1974) However, on the question of whether cohabitation is likely to produce "better" marriages, there is less consensus. Though it is clear that respondents overwhelmingly feel that cohabitation does aid in the ability to choose the right marriage partner, that level of agreement is not found among the researchers.

The implication is clear that Macklin believes that this type of premarital arrangement can certainly be beneficial in choosing a compatible mate. Montgomery, in his assessment of the effect on marriage, is more emphatic in his belief that cohabitation can have a positive effect. He states,

> Couples that live together during courtship will probably make
> fewer mistakes in selecting marriage partners. Their marriage,
> in all probability, will be more reasoned and there will be
> fewer illusions about the person with whom marriage is to take
> place. (Montgomery, 1973:291)

Whitehurst, however, is more skeptical about the usefulness of cohabitation in mate selection. He concludes:

It is no doubt true that most living together unmarried people believe that they will have better marriages for having engaged in this behaviour. There is not so much as one shred of evidence to support this claim. It may simply be that good marriage adjustment depends on other factors-- and that it is so rare in this kind of culture (without essential religious and community supports and with high economic and personal expectations) that it is asking too much of any mate selection system to do this. It may be that no human relationship can endure over as many years as we now expect it to and be anywhere as near fulfilling as we expect. In short, there is a budding folklore of LTU (that it is better than, different from, or helps make better marriages) that may have little basis in reality. (Whitehurst, 1973:11-12, underline added)

This dissertation indicates that most of these cohabiting couples still view marriage as a very serious once-in-a-lifetime step. It is in the interests of establishing a stable marriage that many of these people live together.

The respondents clearly felt that cohabitation created an environment which best enabled them to learn about how they would interact as a married couple. It provided a period of mutual socialization prior to marriage that is not in any way comparable to the traditional custom fo "courtship." The individuals have an opportunity to view each other in realistic day-to-day situations. This helps them to realize that compromise and tolerance are necessary aspects of successful relationships. As a result of this, it becomes easier to reconcile their initial romantic expectations with the practical experience of being together Wednesday morning as well as Saturday night. It appears that young people today are less likely to trust the romantic ideal of marriage. Instead they are more likely to attempt to assume the responsibility for discovering their level of compatability before they make a "permanent" commitment. (Danziger, 1975)

Although the empirical data, testing whether premarital cohabitation would minimize incompatible marriages is not yet available, Spanier (1972) suggests that poor marital adjustment among newly married couples is a function of ideological or romantic notions. If this is found to be true, cohabitation could serve as a means of reducing these notions and perhaps increase the potential for marital stability among those cohabiting couples who do marry.

Though it is yet uncertain whether marriages of couples who have previously lived with each other will be more successful, it is my opinion that the changes for a more stable, permanent wedlock are increased. In addition to the fact that the two individuals have been able to acquire greater knowledge about each other, it is broadly accepted by sociologists that the older people are at first marriage, the greater their chances are for success; and cohabitation is apparently correlated with delaying of marriage. In the words of one female respondent, "It's more than a warm bed at night. I think we both have a much better idea of what marriage is all about."

Perhaps the most positive aspect of cohabitation is that it aids in preventing those marriages between two people who are clearly incompatible.

It seems clear that cohabitation is becoming more prevalent, and it is quite likely to continue to become a more acceptable premarital practive. It is not so clear, however, what the impact on marriage will be in the future. Respondents in this study and others still maintain a view that cohabitation is different from marriage, and the vast majority do expect to be married.

Continued research will be needed to see whether significant changes in marriage can be causally linked to unmarried heterosexual cohabitation. However, we may expect that we will see later marriages, perhaps more egalitarianism, as well as a less romanticized conception of marriage.

The preceding analysis views cohabitation (as the data indicates) as a part of the institution of courtship rather than as a permanent alternative to marriage and the family. If this is so, then it is possible to view the direct implications of cohabitation for the family as minimal. According to Montgomery,

> Cohabitation does not signal the decline of the family; it does not even mean that the family is undergoing rapid and extreme change.... Cohabitation as the means whereby two people live together until they have children will also have a negligible effect on the family. (Montgomery, 1973:295)

In effect, Montgomery asserts, and I would agree, that the growth of the phenomenon of unmarried geterosexual cohabitation does not in itself indicate a decline of the family.

As was indicated above, cohabitants do not expect to have children without marriage. If the purpose of marriage is to create a secure and stable family in which children can be nutured, then cohabitation as an improved form of courtship can be seen as having a positive effect in that it may help to insure better marriages. My feeling is, at this point in time, that the essential nature of the family as security for children is not negatively affected by premarital and pre-child bearing cohabitation. However, it would be near-sighted to suggest that the factors which generated increased adaptation of a life style including cohabitation will not have some effect on family life.

Others have analyzed the effect of our changing society on the institution of the family, and one cannot attempt all things in one study. However, the longer life span, the separation of sexuality from conception and the increasing demands for education and training generate the delaying of marriage.

This delaying of marriage will probably lead to depressed birth rates, an increase in the level of sexual equality, an increase in the autonomy of the adult members of the family, and increased freedom from traditional marital restraints.

APPENDIX I

QUESTIONNAIRE

Our study seeks to better understand the individuals and the living situation of the consensual union. We expect that this questionnaire will do more than increase our understanding of the sociology of unmarried couples. Hopefully, you will be provided with a means of reflecting on your own attitudes and behavior. All responses will remain strictly confidential.

Please circle the appropriate answer or fill in a brief statement where necessary. We would appreciate any additional comments that would clarify your responses.

I. Background Information

1. Please indicate sex:

    1. male
    2. female

2. Please indicate present marital status

    1. single   4. divorced
    2. married   5. widowed
    3. separated

3. What was your age at your last birthday? _____

4. Which of the following best characterizes your financial relationship with your parents?

    1. completely independent financially
    2. partially independent financially
    3. financially dependent on parents

5. What is your father's occupation? _____

6. What is your mother's occupation? _____

7. Approximately what is your parents' combined yearly income before taxes?

    1. under $5,000   5. 13,000-16,000   9. 30,000-40,000
    2. 5,000-7,000   6. 16,000-20,000   10. 40,000-50,000
    3. 7,500-10,000   7. 20,000-25,000   11. over $50,000
    4. 10,000-13,000   8. 25,000-30,000

8. In what social class were you raised?

    1. working class   3. upper-middle class
    2. middle class   4. upper class

9. In what social class do you consider yourself now?

    1. working class   3. upper-middle class
    2. middle class   4. upper class

10. Approximately what is <u>your</u> present income before taxes?

    1. none   5. 7,500-10,000   9. over 20,000
    2. under $3,000   6. 10,000-12,500
    3. 3,000-5,000   7. 12,500-16,000
    4. 5,000-7,500   8. 15,000-20,000

11. What was the last grade of school that you completed? _____
    In what year did you complete your education? _____

12. Please indicate your religious preference:

    1. Catholic   5. atheist
    2. Protestant   6. none
    3. Jewish   7. other _____
    4. agnostic   (please specify)

13. Please indicate your parents' religious preference:

    1. Catholic   5. atheist
    2. Protestant   6. none
    3. Jewish   7. other _____
    4. agnostic   (please specify)

14. How important do you consider religion in your daily life?

    1. very important
    2. moderately important
    3. not important

15. In what size community did you spend your childhood?

    1. small town (under 10,000 pop.)
    2. medium sized town (10,000-25,000)
    3. small city (25,000-80,000)
    4. medium sized city (30,000-200,000)
    5. large city (over 200,000)

16. How close were you to a metropolitan area? _____

17. How many brothers _____ and sisters _____ do you have?
    brothers' ages ___ ___ ___ ___ sisters' ages ___ ___ ___ ___

18. How would you characterize yourself politically?
    (Check one in each column)

    ___Democrat   ___Conservative
    ___Republican   ___Moderate
    ___Independent   ___Liberal
                         ___Radical

19. How would you characterize your parents politically?

    ___Democrat   ___Conservative
    ___Republican   ___Moderate
    ___Independent   ___Liberal
                         ___Radical

20. What was your class standing in high school?

    1. top 10%   4. 50-75%
    2. 10-25%   5. lower quarter
    3. 25-50%

21. If in college or have finished college, what was/is your major
    subject?_____

22. What occupation do you expect to be in five years from now?
    _____
    _____

23. What is your occupation at this time? _____

24. While you were living with your parents, were they ever:

    1. divorced   3. widowed
    2. separated   4. none of the above

25. Would you classify your parents' marriage as:

    1. very happy   4. unhappy
    2. happy   5. very unhappy
    3. neither happy nor unhappy
    comments: _____
    _____

26. How important is privacy to you?

    1. extremely important   3. not very important
    2. important   4. unimportant

27. Did you have enough privacy as a child?

    1. more than enough   3. not enough
    2. a sufficient amount
    comments: _____
    _____

28. How many close friends do you have? _____

29. Would you prefer to have more close friends? 1. yes
                                                  2. no

30. How much respect do you have for your parents?

    1. a great deal   3. little
    2. some   4. none

31. What would you have to do before your parents financially cut you off?
    _____

32. What would you have to do before your parents emotionally cut you off?
    _____

33. Put a check in front of the drugs you consider harmful:

   ___marijuana, hash   ___cocaine, opium
   ___LSD (hallucinogenics)   ___heroin
   ___speed (amphetamines)   ___tranquilizers

34. Has college changed your moral values? _____ If so, please explain:

_____

_____

35. Indicate your feelings about each of the following statements by checking only one of the following for each statement:

Strongly Agree (SA)   Agree (A)   Disagree (D)   Strongly Disagree (SD)

1. Children owe love and respect to their parents.
   SA___ A___ N___ D___ SD___

2. Parents owe love and respect to their children.
   SA___ A___ N___ D___ SD___

3. The traditional family form does not meet the needs of its members.
   SA___ A___ N___ D___ SD___

4. Regular church attendance is an important feature of life.
   SA___ A__ N___ D___ SD___

5. Sex is fun and healthy and should be viewed as just that.
   SA___ A___ N___ D___ SD___

6. Parents try harder to understand their children than children do to understand their parents.
   SA___ A__ N___ D___ SD___

7. Young people who rebel against their society are just going through a stage.
   SA___ A___ N___ D___ SD___

8. Living together improves your ability to choose the right marriage partner.
   SA___ A___ N___ D___ SD___

9. Our present political structure affords maximum individual freedom of choice to everyone.
   SA__ A___ N___ D___ SD___

10. There's nothing wrong with an individual over 18 smoking marijuana in private.
   SA___ A___ N___ D___ SD___

11. Young people are freer than their parents.
   SA___ A___ N___ D___ SD___

12. Sex without love is permissible.
   SA___ A___ N___ D___ SD___

13. Couples living together unmarried is a realistic alternative to the traditional family.
   SA___ A___ N___ D___ SD___

14. Young people are a strong influence on the values and attitudes of their parents.
   SA___ A___ N___ D___ SD___

15. New Jersey should legalize abortions.
SA___ A___ N___ D___ SD___

16. People living together should receive the same tax benefits
as those who are married.
SA___ A___ N___ D___ SD___

17. The state should legalize the concept of renewable marriages.
(i.e., 3 yr. marriage contracts)
SA___ A___ N___ D___ SD___

18. Women should have equal pay, equal job opportunities and equal legal
status in all areas but they should also remain feminine.
SA___ A___ N___ D___ SD___

19. Most of the leaders of the Women's Liberation Movement make anti-male
statements because they have been rejected by the men in their lives.
SA___ A___ N___ D___ SD___

20. Bisexuality is a very natural phenomenon.
SA___ A___ N___ D___ SD___

21. Women should be free to be as affectionate with their women friends
as they are with their men friends.
SA___ A___ N___ D___ SD___

22. If you live with someone and the relationship ends, it becomes more
difficult the next time to be completely open emotionally.
SA___ A___ N___ D___ SD___

23. When two people are secure in their relationship a marriage
contract is unnecessary.
SA___ A___ N___ D___ SD___

24. It is unrealistic to think that two people can live together happily
for their whole lives and achieve optimum personal growth.
SA___ A___ N___ D___ SD___

25. Communal living is the only realistic alternative to the disaster
of the nuclear family in America.
SA___ A___ N___ D___ SD___

26. Divorce should be much easier to accomplish.
SA___ A___ N___ D___ SD___

II.

1. Do you live in an apartment by yourselves? 1. yes   2. no   If not,
please describe your living situation._____

_____

2. Please name the town or city in which you live and in a phrase describe
your immediate community or neighborhood. _____

_____

3. Could you describe the ideal community in which you would like to live,
according to the following characteristics, assuming you remain in the
U.S.A.
a) Section of country (i.e., northeast, south, west)
b) Size of community (i.e., population)_____

c) Type of community (i.e., rural, suburban, urban)
d) Type of housing (i.e., apartment, private house, mobile home, etc)_____
e) Would you prefer your neighbors to be primarily the same age group as you or would you prefer a diverse group?_____
f) Would you prefer an ethnically mixed neighborhood or a homogeneous community?_____
g) Would you prefer an economically homogeneous community or an economically integrated community? _____
h) How important is it for the life styles of your neighbors to be similar to your life style?
___extremely important   ___fairly important
___very important   ___unimportant

4. How long have you lived together? _____

5. Have their been any significant interruptions? Yes___   No___   If yes, how long and why? _____

6. Which of the following statements best describes your relationship?

   a)___We are living together, but ours is not an exclusive relationship; both of us also date other people and our plans for the future are vague.
   b)___We are living together and for the time being our relationship is exclusive. However, our plans for the future are vague.
   c)___We consider our relationship to be very stable and we can foresee living together for some time into the future.
   d)___We consider our relationship a trial marriage.
   e)___We consider our relationship an alternative to marriage.
   f)___None of the above. (Please describe your relationship.) _____
_____

7. Have you ever lived with anyone else in an unmarried couple relationship? Yes___   No___   If yes, how many different people have you lived with and for what periods of time? _____

8. Have you ever been married? Yes___   No___
If yes, for how long? _____
If you have been involved in a marriage that ended, what do you feel was the primary reason? _____

9. Do you have any children? Yes___   No___
If yes, how many? _____   How old are they? _____

10. Would you describe in a sentence or two the main reasons that influenced your decision to live together? _____
_____

11. Upon entering the relationship were any rules of behavior decided upon? If so, describe _____
_____

12. Upon entering the relationship were any commitments made? If so, what were they? _____
_____

13. How long did you have a relationship before you started living together?
_____

14. How and where did you meet? _____

15. Do you think you will eventually marry the person you're living with?
Yes___ No___ Cannot say at this time___

16. Do you think you will eventually marry anyone?
Yes___ No___ Cannot say at this time___

17. Does the subject of marriage come up often between you and the person
you're living with? Yes___ No___

18. If you found you were expecting a child, what would you do? (Get married,
have an abortion, etc.) _____

19. How important is sex in your relationship?
1.___extremely important   3.___fairly important
2.___very important   4.___unimportnat
If other, please specify _____

20. Do you think that unmarried couples should have children? Yes___ No___
Why or why not? _____

21. Do your parents know that you are living together? Yes___ No___ If yes,
a) how do they feel about it? _____
b) if not, why not? _____ _____

22. Do your parents ever visit both of you? Yes___ No___

23. Do you two ever visit your parents together? Yes___ No___

24. If your parents are aware of your living situation, has your relationship
with them been affected? Yes___ No___ Comments:_____

25. If your parents are aware of your living situation, has your relationship
with the person you are living with been affected? Yes___ No___
Comments: _____

26. Psychologists argue that involving oneself in behavior not totally
accepted by the society may produce feelings of guilt. Does this in
any way apply to your relationship? _____

27. Do your grandparents know you are living together? Yes___ No___

28. Do your aunts and uncles know? Yes___ No___

29. Do your friends know? Yes___ No___

30. Do your work associates or fellow students know? Yes___ No___

31. Do your neighbors know you're living together without marriage? Yes__ No__

32. Do you attend family functions together where relatives are aware of your living situation? Yes___ No___ Comments: _____

33. What are the advantages of living together? _____
_____

34. What are the disadvantages? _____
_____

35. What do you feel are the advantages of traditional marriage? _____
_____

36. What are the disadvantages of traditional marriage? _____
_____

37. Do you as an individual feel you have enough privacy? Yes___ No___

39. If certain topics or issues lead to disagreements between you and your partner, please describe them. _____

40. Do you use any of the following drugs?

	Yes	No
marijuana, hash	___	___
LSD (hallucenogenics)	___	___
speed (amphetamines)	___	___
cocaine, opium	___	___
heroin	___	___
tranquilizers	___	___

41. If you use any of the above drugs, approximately how often? _____

42. Have you made any plans for the future in terms of your relationship? Please explain _____

43. What could cause the relationship to end? _____

44. During the week how many hours a day do you spend with each other? (Include sleep time) _____

45. On weekends how many hours a day do you spend with each other? (Include sleep time) _____

46. Do you take separate vacations? Yes___ No___ Comments: _____

47. In what ways do you spend your own leisure time? _____

48. In what ways do you spend leisure time with your partner? _____

49. Financial arrangements: Please check the appropriate category. Who pays for the following?

	I Pay	Partner Pays	Share	No Specific Arrangm.
Rent	___	___	___	___
Food	___	___	___	___
Household items	___	___	___	___

49. continued

	I Pay	Partner Pays	Share	No Specific Arrangm.
Appliances (TV, etc.)	____	____	____	____
Clothing	____	____	____	____
Gas & Electric	____	____	____	____

50. Who is making more money? _____

51. Do you keep your money in the same bank account? Yes___ No___

52. What types of things are you typically responsible for? (i.e., cooking, cleaning, taking out the garbage, etc.) _____

53. Did you have more or less difficulties in living together than you had expected? More ___ Less ___ Comments:_____

54. Do you think people living together have obligations to each other? Yes___ No___ If yes, what are they? _____

55. Do these obligations limit your own personal freedom? Yes___ No___ Please comment: _____

56. Do you think the number of poeple living together without marriage will grow significantly over the next 30 years? Yes___ No___ Why or why not? _____

57. Do you think the government will find means of legalizing living together without a traditional marriage contract? Yes___ No___

58. Recently a bill introduced in the Pennsylvania State Sentate proposed the creation of a 3 year (renewable) marriage contract. Do you think many people would take advantage of this? Yes___ No___

59. Would you be interested in this alternative? Yes___ No___

60. What changes would you like to see, or additions would you like to make, to our marriage laws? _____

61. Do the two of you share a similar political ideology? Yes___ No___ Please explain _____

62. Do the two of you share similar personal philosophy (how to live one's life)? Yes___ No___ Please explain_____

63. Do you expect to maintain a lasting relationship? Definitely ___ Probably___ Unsure___ No___

64. When you think about the relationship in which you live, do you think
   a)___Living together without marriage is the only situation in which you can be happy.
   b)___You feel happy living together but probably would feel as happy if the relationship was institutionalized (marriage).

c)___There are other living situations in which you would feel happier. If so please specify (i.e., commune, marriage, living alone, living with parents) _____

d)___You are unhappy about living together. Why? _____

65. How many of your friends are living together in a similar way?_____

66. In most cases of which you are aware, how has the situation worked out?
_____

67. If you had to write one sentence to describe your relationship, what would you say? _____
_____

APPENDIX II

INTERVIEW SCHEDULE

1. Please describe how and why you started a living together relationship (i.e., please give me a brief history of your relationship).

    What did you think were the advantages of living together?

    How have things worked out?

    Was it the way you expected?

    What did you see as the negative consequence of living together?

    What has your experience shown you?

2. What are the goals of your living together?

    For you?

    For the couple?

    Have you achieved these goals?

    Does marriage have anything to do with the purpose of your cohabitation?

    Do you expect to marry the person you are living with?

    Anyone?

    Is cohabitation just like marriage?

3. Are there any rules of behavior that you established before you started living together or that have evolved since that time?

    What happens when these rules are broken?

    Can you describe a specific example?

    Is your relationship monogamous?

    Did you explicitly or implicitly set up any rules concerning sexual fidelity?

    What would happen (or has happened) to your relationship if you (your partner) had a sexual relationship with someone else?

4. What are the areas in which you and your partner disagree?

    How do you resolve these differences?

5. How long did you expect to live together when you first started cohabiting?

   How long do you expect to live together now?

   How has your relationship changed since you started living together?

   What might cause the relationship to end?

   Why aren't you married?

   How would that change the relationship?

6. Do your parents know you are living together?

   How did they find out about your living arrangements?

   Did you make any attempt to conceal your relationship from them?

   How do they feel about what you are doing?

   Do they try to influence you in any way concerning your relationship with _____?

   Has your relationship with your parents been affected by your cohabitation with _____?

   Has your relationship with _____been affected by any reaction on the part of your parents?

   Are other members of the family aware of your living situation?

   Do your parents visit the two of you?

   Do you visit them?

   Do you sleep together when visiting?

7. Is cohabitation the best way to find a good marriage partner or is marriage itself an obsolete institution?

   Do you think that living together before marriage should be required of any couple who wants to get married?

   Why do you think people (college students) are living together more now than they did 10 years ago?

8. Have you ever been involved in a living together relationship before?

   What happened to that relationship(s)?

   Please breifly describe how you got together? how long were you together? why the relationship did not continue?

Do you still see each other?

Was the break up difficult?

Did you think you would live with another person again?

Did it have any effect on your views of marriage (or living together)?

SELECTED BIBLIOGRAPHY

Arafat, Ibithaj and Betty Yorburg
    1973   "On living together without marriage."
                 Journal of Sex Research (May):97-106.

Bell, Robert R.
    1971   Social Deviancy. Home wood, Illinois:
                 Dorsey Press.

Bell, Robert R. and Jay B. Chaskes
    1970   "Premarital sexual experience among coeds,
                 1958 and 1968." Journal of Marriage and the
                 Family (February):81-84.

Berger, Miriam E.
    1971   "Trial marriage: harnessing the trend
                 constructively." The Family Coordinator
                 20:38-43.

Blumer, Herbert
    1969   Symbolic Interactionism. Englewood Cliffs,
                 New Jersey: Prentice Hall.

Bolton, Charles D.
    1961   "Mate selection as the development of a
                 relationship." Marriage and Family Living
                 23:234-240.

Cadwallader, Mervyn
    1966   "Marriage as a wretched institution."
                 Atlantic Monthly 218 5:62-66.

Clatworthy, Nancy M.
    1975   "Couples in quasi-marriage." In Nona Glazer-
                 Malgin (ed.), Old Family/New Family: Inter-
                 personal Relationships. New York: Van Nostrand.

Cole, Charles
    1973   "Emerging dating and intimacy requirements of
                 a midwestern university: a study of cohabitation
                 and other alternative courtship forms."
                 Unpublished manuscript, Denison Universtiy,
                 Granville, Ohio.

Coleman, James
    1970   "Relational analysis: the study of social
                 organization with survey methods." PP. 118-119
                 in Norman K. Denzin, Sociological Methods.
                 Chicago: Aldine.

Danziger, Carl
    1973   "Does living together make better marriages."
               Human Sexuality. New York: Hospital Publications, Inc.

Danziger, Carl
    1971   "Alternatives to the family." Unpublished paper.

Danziger, Carl and Mathew Greenwald
    1973   Alternatives: A Look at Unmarried Couples and
               Communes. New York: Research Services, Institute
               of Life Insurance, 277 Park Avenue.

Driscoll, Richard, Keith Davis and Milton Lipitz
    1970   "Parental interference and romantic love:
               the Romeo and Juliet effect." In Journal
               of Personality and Social Psychology.

Erikson, Erik H.
    1959   "The problem of ego identity." In Identity
               and the Life Cycle. Published as Vol. I,
               No. 1 of Psychological Issues.

    1963   Youth: Change and Challenge. New York: Basic Books, Inc.

Farber, Bernard
    1964   Family: Organization and Interaction.
               San Francisco: Chandler Publishing Co.

Farson, Richard E.
    1969   The Future of the Family. New York:
               Family Service Association.

Fielding, William J.
    1961   Strange Customs of Courtship and Marriage.
               London: Souvenir Press.

Flacks, Richard
    1971   Youth and Social Change.
               Chicago: Markham Publishing Co.

Garza, Joseph
    1974   "Living together and the double funnel theory
               of courtship." Paper presented at Fourth Annual
               Sociological Research Symposium, Virginia Commonwealth
               University, Richmond, Virginia, February 28-March 2.

Gibney, Frank
    1948   "The strange ways of Staphorst." Life (September 27):2-8.

Henze, Lura F. and John W. Hudson
    1974   "Personal and family characteristics of non-cohabiting
               college students." Journal of Marriage and the Family (May).

Houser, Philip
    1969   "Social science predicts and projects." In
                Richard E. Farson, The Future of the Family.
                New York: Family Service Association.

Hudson, John W. and Lura F. Henze
    1973   "A note on cohabitation."
                The Family Coordinator (October):495.

Johnson, Michael P.
    1973   "Commitment: a conceptual structure and
                empirical application." Sociological
                Quarterly (Summer)14:395-406.

Kalmbach, Carla
    1973   "Replication study of heterosexual cohabitation
                among unmarried college students: Cornell University
                vs. Central Michigan Universtiy." Unpublished manuscript.

Keniston, Kenneth
    1965   The Uncommitted. New York: Harcourt, Brace and World.

    1971   Youth and Dissent. New York: Harcourt, Brace, Janovich, Inc.

Kerckhoff, Alan C. and Keith Davis
    1962   "Value consensus and need complementarity in
                mate selection." American Sociological Review 27:295-303.

Lautenschlager, Sheryl Y.
    1972   "A descriptive study of consensual union among
                college students." Unpublished Masters Thesis,
                California State University, Northridge, California, 1972.

Lewinsohn, Richard
    1958   The History of Sexual Customs. New York: Harper Brothers.

Lewis, Robert A.
    1972   "A developmental framework for the analysis of premarital
                dyadic formation." Family Process 11 (March):17-48.

    1973   "A longitudinal test of a developmental framework for
                premarital dyadic formation." Journal or Marriage and
                the Family 35 (February):16-25.

Lindsey, Ben B. and Evans Wainright
    1927   The Companionate Marriage. New York: Boni and Live.

    1927   "The companionate marriage." Redbook (October).

Lyness, Judith L., Milton E. Kipetz and Keith E. Davis
    1972   "Living together: an alternative to marriage." Journal
                of Marriage and the Family 34 (May):305-311.

Mace, David
    1958   Success in Marriage. Nashville, Tennessee: Abingdon Press.

Macklin, Eleanor D.
    1971   "Heterosexual cohabitation among unmarried college
                students." Unpublished working paper presented at
                Groves Conference on Marriage and the Family, May 7-10.

    1972   "Heterosexual cohabitation among unmarried college
                students." The Family Coordinator (October)463-472.

    1972-   Cohabitation Research Newsletter 1-4.
    1974

    1974   "Unmarried heterosexual cohabitation on the university
                campus." Unpublished manuscript, Cornell University,
                Ithaca, New York.

MacLean, C.
    1941   "Trial marriage among the Peruvian Aborigines."
                Mexican Sociology 1:25-33 (in Spanish).

Malmowski, Bronislaw
    1929   The Sexual Life of Savages. London: George Routledge and Sons.

Mazur, Ronald
    1973   "Beyond jealousy and possessiveness." In
                Rogers W. Libby and Robert N. Whitehurst,
                Renovating Marriage. Danville, California:
                Consensus Publishers.

McCall, M.M.
    1966   "Courtship as a social exchange: some historical
                comparisons." Pp. 190-200 in B. Farber (ed.), Kinship
                and Family Organization. New York: Wiley.

Mead, Margaret
    1966   "Marriage in two steps." Redbook (July):48.

    1968   "A continuing dialogue on marriage: why just living
                together won't work." Redbook (April):44.

    1970   Culture and Commitment: A Study of the Generation Gap.
                New York: Doubleday.

Montgomery, Jason P.
    1973   "Towards an understanding of cohabitation." Unpublished
                Ph.D thesis, University of Massachusetts, Amherst, Mass.

Moore, Allen J.
    1969   The Young Adult Generation. Nashville: Abington Press.

Nasholm, Astrid
    1972   "Married cohabitation and unmarried cohabitation"
               and "The parent study by the State Insurance
               Company." SOU:41.

Newsweek
    1966   "Unstructured relationships: students living
               together." (July 4):78.

O'Neill, Nena and George
    1972   Open Marriage. New York: M. Evans, Inc.

Parsons, Talcott and Gerald M. Platt
    1972   "Higher education and changing socialization."
               In Matilda White Riley, et al., Aging and Society.
               New York: Russell Sage Foundation.

Peterman, Dan J., Carl A. Ridley and Scott M. Anderson
    1974   "A comparison of cohabiting and non-cohabiting
               college sutdents." Journal of Marriage and the
               Family 36 (May):344-354.

Rapoport, Rhona
    1963   "Normal crises, family structure and mental health."
               Family Process (March)2:68-80.

Reiss, Ira L.
    1960   "Toward a sociology of the heterosexual love
               relationship." Marriage and Family Living 22:139-145.

    1967   The Social Context of Premarital Permissiveness.
               New York: Holt, Rinehart and Winston.

Riley, Matilda White
    1963   Sociological Research I - A Case Approach.
               New York: Harcourt, Brace and World, Inc.

Russell, Bertrand
    1929   Marriage and Morals. New York: Liverright.

    1971   "On marriage." Pp. 283-286 in Arlene S. and Jerome H.
               Skolnick (eds.), Family in Stransition.
               Boston: Little, Brown and Co.

Safire, William
    1937   "On cohabitation." New York Times (September):31M.

Satire, Virginia
    1967   "Marriage as a statutory five year renewable contract."
               Paper presented at the American Psychological Association
               Annual Convention, Washington, D.C., September 1.

Schrag, Peter
    1968   "Posse at generation gap: implications of the Linda
              LeClair affair." Saturday Review (May 18):81.

Scott, George Tyley
    1960   Marriage - An Inquiry Relating to all Races and Nations
              From Antiquity to Present Day. New York: Key Publishing Co.

Scriven, Michael
    1968   "Putting the sex back into sex education."
              Phi Delta 49(9).

Selltiz, Claire, et al.
    1959   Research Methods in Social Relations.
              New York: Henry Holt and Co., Inc.

Shuttlesworth, Buy and George Thorman
    1973   "Living together unmarried relationships."
              Unpublished manuscript, University of Texas, Austin, Texas.

Slater, Philip
    1970   The Pursuit of Loneliness. Boston: Beacon Press.

Spanier, Graham B.
    1972   "Romanticism and marital adjustment." Journal of
              Marriage and the Family. (August)34:481-437.

Stephenson, Richard M.
    1973   "Involvement in deviance: an example and some
              theoretical implications." Social Problems.

Stiles, Henry Reed
    (1971)   Bundling:Its Origin, Progress and Decline in America.
    1934   New York: Cook Collectors Association, Inc.

Time
    1968   "Linda, the light housekeeper." (April 26):51.

    1970   "The American family: future uncertain." (December 28):34.

Toffler, Alvin
    1970   Future Shock. New York: Random House.

Trost, Jan
    1974   "Various forms of cohabitation and their relation to
              psychical and social criteria of adaptation." Paper
              presented at the Eighth World Congress of Sociology,
              Committee on Family Research, Toronto, Canada, August
              18-24. (Mineographed).

Wells, Theodora and Lee S. Christie
    1970   "Living together: an alternative to marriage."
              The Futurist (April)4:50-51.

Weinberg, Martin S.

    1968   "Sexual modesty and the nudist camp" and "Becoming a nudist." In Earl Rubington and Martin S. Weinberg, Deviance: The Interactionist Perspective. New York: The Macmillan Co.

Whitehurst, Robert N.

    1969   "The unmalias on campus." Unpublished manuscript presented at NCFR Annual Meeting.

    1973   "Living together unmarried: some trends and speculation." Unpublished manuscript, University of Windsor, Windsor, Ontario.

    1974   "Sex-role equality and changing meanings in cohabitation." Unpublished manuscript.

Yankelovich, Daniel

    1972   Changing Values on Campus. New York: Washington Square Press.

    1974   Changing Youth Values in the 70's: A Study of American Youth. New York: McGraw Hill.